PITT SERIES IN NATURAL HISTORY

ALSO BY MARCIA BONTA

Escape to the Mountain
Outbound Journeys in Pennsylvania
Women in the Field
Appalachian Spring

Appalachian Autumn

MARCIA BONTA

University of Pittsburgh Press

PITTSBURGH AND LONDON

Published by the University of Pittsburgh Press, Pittsburgh, Pa. 15260

Manufactured in the United States of America

Printed on acid-free paper

LIBRARY OF CONGRESS CATALOGING-IN-PUBLICATION DATA

Bonta, Marcia, 1940–
    Appalachian autumn / Marcia Bonta.
       p. cm. — (Pitt series in nature and natural history)
    Includes bibliographical references (p.) and index.
    ISBN 0-8229-3784-0 (cl). — ISBN 0-8229-5534-2 (pbk.)
    1. Natural history—Appalachian Region. 2. Forest ecology—
Appalachian Region. 3. Autumn—Appalachian Region.
4. Clearcutting—Environmental aspects—Appalachian Region.
I. Title. II. Series.
QH104.5.A6B65 1994
508.748—dc20   94-10161
                                            CIP

A CIP catalogue record for this book is available from the British Library.

Eurospan, London

Portions of this book first appeared, in slightly different form, in the *Altoona Mirror, Bird Watcher's Digest, Birder's World, Hawk Mountain News, Pennsylvania Game News,* and *Wild Bird.*

The map on p. 2 was prepared by Mark Bonta and Bill Nelson.

To my husband Bruce
who never gave up and to those who helped us,
Ned, Bill, Duff, Teddy, and Bob.

PLUMMER'S HOLLOW ELEGY

(In Memoriam, February 12, 1992)

when her mind went they took her away
from the house in the hollow where she'd lived
forty years like a hermit
with her dog and her shotgun a color tv
and her dead brother's artificial legs standing
guard at the top of the stairs

her ancestors' land had been sold out from under her
and clearcut by the absentee owner
who couldn't be bothered with a mother's deathbed
   commandment
half a century old:
Let no one lumber the mountain again.
she'll never survive a third cutting
and neither will you.

                         DAVID BONTA

Contents

Introduction

THIS BOOK was to be a praise-song for an Appalachian autumn, full of the happenings and special beauties of this loveliest of Pennsylvania's seasons, and so it is. But autumn is a bittersweet time, a reminder that in life there is death and in death life as the natural system partially shuts down after a spectacular season of harvest and fulfillment. Most of the birds flee south, many animals hibernate or sleep away a good portion of late autumn and winter, and the last wildflowers wither and die. It is a season of good-byes, when, after the flaming leaves fall and start the inevitable process of decay, we are left with only the bare bones of nature. Those natural companions who can neither migrate nor hibernate—the deer and turkeys, ruffed grouse and rabbits, squirrels and songbirds, foxes and coyotes—become more visible, so autumn is a good time for wildlife watching. The weather can be warm and beguiling, most of the biting insects are gone, and the clear, crisp days bring out the wanderlust in me.

It is easy to move through the woods, walking miles along the ridgetop, stopping to sit with my back against a tree or lying in a bed of newly fallen leaves. As I fade into the background, the animals come alive—turkeys stalk toward me, bent on looking for food; a buck sails past, grunting loudly in hot pursuit of a doe; and chipmunks chase each other with such concentration that they run over my outstretched legs, thinking they are just two more fallen tree branches. Red, fox, and gray squirrels are busily harvesting whatever acorns have fallen and barely notice me.

But other sounds and sights frequently disturb my reveries. Those are made by man, the harvester. In the valley below and on the mountainside, I can hear the noise of tractors, of guns, and of chain saws as farmers gather in their crops, hunters harvest wild meat, and woodlot owners cut their winter heating supply—all too a part of the natural cycle. Once, when we were young, we also grew most of our food, killed animals for meat, and cut our dead trees for firewood. Like most Americans, however, we have gradually let others supply those basic needs. Still, we understand the desires of many of our neighbors to harvest the surplus as long as they are careful not to take too much or to destroy the basis for their productivity—the soil, water, and wildlife. Those resources belong to everyone, and if they are destroyed, we will be destroyed too.

Unfortunately, though, many landowners consider what they do to their property to be their own business, even if it impacts their neighbors. That has been the situation here for most of the years we have lived on our wooded mountaintop, particularly in autumn when, several times, adjacent landowners decided not to harvest their woodlots sustainably, but to either take off all the big trees or, in the worst-case scenario, to clear-cut the steep mountain slopes with no thought of those living below. So the sound of chain saws, even those used by people who are cutting firewood, sends me into a panic. Who is cutting now and where? Must we again try to stop the irresponsible rape of the forest?

For thirteen years we have been fighting loggers who threatened our access road. In our innocence we bought this property—150 acres, more or less, of mountaintop land—in 1971 and never stopped to ask who owned the land on either side of our primitive, mile-and-a-half access road. For seven years we lived in peace with our elderly neighbors, Margaret and her brother Fred. We knew that they did not own their land and home, but Margaret often said that she had promised her mother never to cut the trees on what had once been their family's property. We assumed she had enough influence on the landowner, a businessman from Kentucky, to keep those 120 acres safe.

However, shortly after Fred died in the winter of 1977–78, we began a three-year battle along with Margaret to protect the road and the lowest portion of the hollow from a planned clear-cut by another absentee owner. My husband, Bruce, led the battle. He elicited the support of an engineering professor in his struggle to reduce the weight limit on the county bridge over the river that provides access to our road. We had several meetings with attorneys and the county commissioners about the matter. Bruce also talked with officials in the state's Department of Environmental Resources about maintaining the purity of the stream in Plummer's Hollow, which flows into the Little Juniata River at the base of the mountain.

But the critical issue was the threat to our road, our lifeline to the outside, posed by the use of heavy equipment on or near it. Our fears about the effects of lumbering directly above the road on the steep mountain slopes were confirmed by a geologist on the faculty of the university. He explained that a major lineament, a type of fault, stretched for miles along the river valley, and it was surrounded along its entire length by a maze of smaller lineaments and fracture traces which etched the mountains and valleys within a couple of miles on either side. These lineaments and fracture traces conduct water and cause landslides, he explained, wherever the earth is disturbed. Even minor disturbances to the forest directly above our road in the hollow where these lineaments and fracture traces crossed might produce small earth slides that would take out our road.

After much negotiation, the logger who had been hired to clear-cut the property agreed to attend a meeting with several state officials and the geologist. He listened carefully to the geologist's presentation and decided a few weeks later to withdraw from the job. The landowner then wanted to sell his land, and after a long struggle to clear the titles, we were able to buy the property—one section in 1984 and the other in 1985, but not before the end of the ridge was selectively cut by another logger hired by the landowner.

In 1986, the owner of Margaret's land, the Kentucky businessman, decided he wanted to lumber his property. He hired a local attorney and pressured us about his right to use our road for his timbering operation. Since the lowest portion of the road was now completely on our land, (as of 1985) we were able to prevent this destruction.

That fall the Kentucky businessman sold the property to a lumberman who operated a sawmill twenty-five miles away in the southern end of the county. He indicated a firm determination to cut down the trees on his newly acquired property, but by the autumn of 1991, when I decided to carefully chronicle the daily natural occurrences in the woods, fields, and hollow, the lumbering had still not taken place. The danger to the hollow seemed remote since he had been threatening for years and had not followed through.

In order for the story of the autumn of 1991 to be clear, it is necessary to give a few of the details of our five years of attempts to negotiate with the man. When Bruce first met him and his forester along the road in early 1987 he had been assured that they planned to cut only the big dead trees on his property—and maybe some of the bigger live trees also. The lumberman was friendly and jovial so we were optimistic that a reasonable compromise could be reached.

At a meeting in June, however, when we refused to allow him the use of our road, the lumberman's tone changed considerably. He tried both blustering and bullying us, declaring that our road was a public right of way, and claiming that his property line followed not the road, as both of our deeds indicated, but the stream that flowed about fifty feet below the road. He insisted that he could block us along the four thousand feet of roadway that, he alleged, was completely on his property, and he could put gates along the road to prevent our access.

The forester was as persistent as the lumberman. He insisted that they had the right to cut down to the property line, which they planned to do. Bruce tried to explain about fracture traces and lineaments, and that cutting trees next to or below the road would destroy it, but he got only bland assurances from the forester that they would never harm the road. Since our land now totally surrounded their property, Bruce maintained that, if they wanted permission to skid their logs across our property to the hollow entrance, they would have to agree to stay well above the road in their work. They refused to make such an agreement. The lumberman did reassure us repeatedly that they would never do a clear-cut—that was a terrible way to cut wood. This statement was repeated several times by the forester during subsequent conversations: his boss only did careful, selective cutting jobs and was widely known for the responsible work he did in the woods.

Nearly three years went by, a period of continual efforts by Bruce to reopen negotiations. The forester studied the property deeds and decided that our property did not completely surround theirs, as we had believed. A survey confirmed his claim that there was a 219-foot gap that allowed access to the lumberman's land from a neighbor's property on the highway side of the mountain. At a meeting in our attorney's office in February 1990 the lumberman indicated that, since his right of way through the neighbor's property into his own land was now secure, he would begin cutting immediately. But he would not agree to stay even 200 feet above the road. Desperate to save our access road, I proposed that we agree to a land swap. In exchange for the steep strip of land 200 feet above the road, we would give them comparable acreage on top of the mountain containing roughly an equivalent number of trees. The lumberman seemed eager to compromise this far at least. His forester would do the initial survey of trees on both properties and then share the results by hiking over the area with Bruce. After that, we would hire our own forester to do an estimate of the comparative tree values on both properties. Once this was finished, we would complete the deal by hammering out our differences.

The forester was obviously not happy with the deal—he really did not believe there would be any problem in cutting the trees right down to their property line—but the lumberman seemed pleased. He agreed to my proposal, and as the meeting broke up he said about Bruce, "I like this pup, even if he does give me a lot of trouble."

The forester marked the trees on both properties, and one September morning he and Bruce and our son Steve hiked over the area. Bruce indicated at the end of the walk that he would like to proceed as we had agreed. He wanted to hire his own expert to make calculations for us, and we would share the forester's calculations with the person we hired. They could then get together to resolve any differences. The forester hesitated, but finally said he would talk with his boss about that and get back to us.

Ominously, we heard nothing about the lumbering. In October 1990, Margaret finally decided, because of her advancing age, to leave her lifelong home on the mountain to live with friends in town. During the spring Bruce

tried to press the lumberman to help with road maintenance work—if he had the right to use the road, he had
the obligation to help keep it up—but after a phone call
and several letters were not answered, Bruce gave up trying to work with him. In his last letter to the lumberman
about road maintenance, Bruce threatened to change the
lock on the gate at the entrance to the hollow if he didn't
respond. We heard nothing from him so Bruce finally
changed the lock in late June.

The summer of 1991 was the driest on record, and all
signs pointed to a spectacular autumn ahead. It would be
a perfect year to record an Appalachian autumn—the
wildlife and plants preparing for winter, humanity storing
nature's surplus. The proposed lumbering seemed like a
remote issue.

*Appalachian
Autumn*

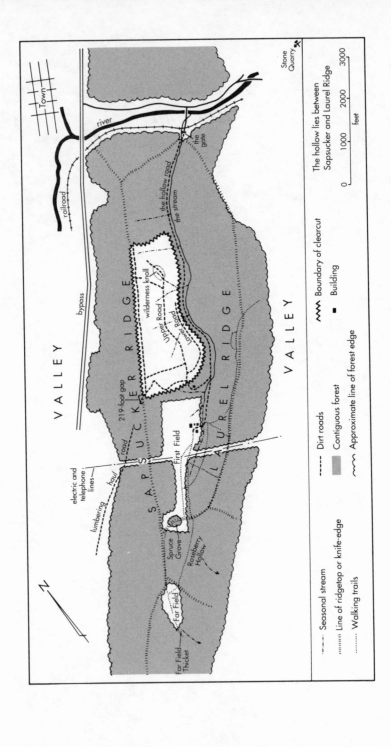

The hollow lies between
Sapsucker and Laurel Ridge

0	1000	2000	3000

feet

Stone Quarry

— · — · — Seasonal stream

— · · — Line of ridgetop or knife-edge

· · · · · · Walking trails

- - - - Dirt roads

〜〜〜 Boundary of clearcut

▪ Building

▨ Contiguous forest

〜〜〜 Approximate line of forest edge

VALLEY

VALLEY

S A P S U C K E R   R I D G E

L A U R E L   R I D G E

Town

river

railroad

bypass

electric and telephone lines

lumbering   haul   road

219-foot gap

Upper Road

Lower Road

wilderness knoll

First Field

Spruce Grove

Roseberry Hollow

Far Field

Far Field Thicket

the hollow road

the stream

the gate

N

Prologue

I've lived on Cold Mountain a little while now—
Already a couple eons have come and gone.
Following my own path I escaped to the woods and streams,
And here I am, still lost in mute wonder.
The icy cliffs keep visitors at bay;
Layers of cloud form an impenetrable curtain.
I make my bed in the deep grass,
Take the clear sky for a quilt;
A rock for my pillow and I'm content
To let the world go about its business.

—Han-Shan (8th century)
translated by David Bonta

Sometime in early August, summer's humidity is blown away for a day or two. Intimations of autumn are in the air. Billowing clouds, pushed along by the cleansing winds, race across the blue sky. The breast-high grasses of First Field seethe and ripple like a restless ocean. Eagerly I scan the sky for migrating raptors, and instead I spot a turkey vulture sporting in the wind, dipping back and forth, up and down, as if for the sheer joy of it.

Such joy is infectious, so I plow through the grasses as if I am swimming and finally reach the overhanging arms of a catalpa tree growing at the top of the field. It provides almost perfect camouflage for me with its huge, heart-shaped leaves and drooping branches which reach within a foot or two of the ground. Peering out from its womblike protection, seeing but unseen, a childish urge comes over me to set up house beneath its translucent, limegreen leaves and watch the world go by.

Later I tell my husband, Bruce, half-jokingly that I am going to spend autumn lying up in First Field, taking notes on the clouds as they whiz by. A confirmed cloud watcher since childhood, he is sympathetic. Clouds, he believes, are fascinating because their fluidity represents another dimension we cannot enter. They take us away from our earthly concerns. Perhaps, I suggest, clouds are angels in disguise, appearing and disappearing like will-o'-the-wisps, full of mystery and change, ephemeral and yet permanent fixtures in the infinite scheme of sky and space. Whatever they may be, the scudding clouds brought me autumn for a day.

Since mid-April barn swallows have swooped over the field, snatching insects from the air to nourish the two broods they raise in our barn. By August, between fifteen and thirty parents and their offspring are lining up on the telephone wire and chattering away, reminding me of gossiping neighbors. Then one day I count fifty barn swallows, the next morning one hundred. Barn swallows are on the move and our telephone wire attracts them like a magnet. The migrants come and go in the misty dawn during the first two weeks of August, but still our residents remain. And then one morning I step outside to silence. They have gone south for the winter, the first of the neotropical migrants to leave us, and for days I am bereft. Those four months they have spent with us seem too little time in the year's scheme. Other birds continue to call and even sing, but they do not have the ineffable charm and joie de vivre of barn swallows. Without them the field has lost its fluidity, and my spirit no longer soars as it does during those months of watching their mastery of the air.

As summer dwindles away, the mountain continues to exhibit signs of the impending change. Here and there the leaves of black gum trees, the earliest to turn color in the woods and the most beautiful, have turned whole branches reddish purple. At the same time, the leaves of black walnut trees in the yard are yellowing, curling up, and sifting to the ground with every vagrant breeze. In First Field the five species of goldenrod and the upland white asters are blooming, while in the woods and along the hollow road I find turtlehead, white wood asters, silverrod, and late-flowering throroughwort—all flowers associated with autumn.

Sometime in early August I hear the high, keening cries of cedar waxwings, and I know the wild black cherries are ripe. Those wandering flocks of birds seem to have super-sensitive antennae that tune them in the instant the cherries are ready. One day the mountain is empty of waxwings, the next they are everywhere. On a bright, blue morning I sit at the top of First Field and watch the wild black cherry treetops surge and pulse with cedar waxwings flying down, up, over, around, as if they cannot contain themselves, cannot settle down to eat, but have to celebrate by exuberant flight like so many over-sized butterflies, their golden breasts flashing in the sunlight.

At the same time the squirrels begin harvesting nuts. The first to mature are the black walnuts. Then, by mid-month, the shagbark hickory nuts have ripened along the Far Field Road. One beautiful morning hickory shell pieces rain down as I walk beneath the trees, and so I sit motionless in the dark woods watching for foraging squirrels among the thick leaf canopy. A gray squirrel approaches, hopping purposefully toward me with a hickory nut in its mouth. It pauses and spots me less than ten feet away. Carefully it backtracks, circling widely, but still unhurried and graceful.

A second gray squirrel crosses the road on an overhanging tree branch, then leaps its way from branch to branch to the hickory trees, stopping to scratch nonchalantly before harvesting a nut. Two more chase and squeal from tree to tree before settling down and gathering their own nuts and finally sitting apart from the other squirrels to eat. Probably they are juveniles trying to avoid harassment by adults. According to Lucia Jacobs, who studied gray squirrels on the Princeton University campus, shagbark hickory nuts are gray squirrels' favorite food. Those squirrels she observed showed preferences for certain trees, and three years in a row they began their fall harvest in the same shagbark hickory. The same is true here. Those two Far Field Road trees draw dozens of feeding squirrels in what sometimes looks like a feeding frenzy, because the squirrels do little storing, eating most of the nuts on site.

Using their jaws like crowbars, they insert their lower incisors into a hole they have gnawed. Then, bit by bit, they break off pieces of hickory shell and expose the nut meat, a process that takes them only a few minutes. Hickory nuts have twice the calories of an acorn and are far tastier, so gray squirrels are not only nutritionists but gourmets. In less than a week, those two trees are stripped of nuts and the ground beneath them is littered with shell pieces. Only then do the squirrels move on to the acorns.

Near the end of August, the first waves of migrating warblers have landed on the mountain to forage. I am alerted as we sit eating breakfast on the front porch and see, suddenly, a flutter of birds high in the tops of the black locust trees in the front yard. First I zero in on a Black-burnian warbler, then by "pish, pish, pishing," my mouth pursed and hissing, I call down black-throated blue, black-throated green, and black-and-white warblers along with a ruby-crowned kinglet into a nearby lilac bush.

Mixed in are all the "confusing fall warblers," as Roger Tory Peterson calls them in his *Field Guide to the Birds of Eastern and Central North America*. Mostly immatures and females, they are duller versions of the males and often lack their distinguishing characteristics, for instance, the flaming orange throat and face stripes of the Blackburnian, the black throat and blue back of the black-throated blue, and the black throat of the black-throated green. Black-and-whites, bless them, are always striped in black and white, and ruby-crowned kinglets, which are not warblers but travel with them, always have distinguishing, broken white eye-rings and white wing bars on their tiny, undistinguished, olive green bodies. Their ruby crowns are rarely visible in the spring and even less so in the fall.

"Real" birders, those folks with keen eyes and a competitive streak, relish the challenge fall warblers present to their identification skills. I, with my middle-aged eyesight and slower reflexes, dismiss them with a sigh as "nondescript" and allow them to proceed unidentified but not unappreciated.

The raptor migration, too, is well on its way by the end of August. First to appear are the northern harriers, hunting low over First Field. Formerly called marsh hawks because of their preferred habitat, they are satisfying birds to identify because the gray-backed males, brown-backed females, and russet-breasted immatures hunt close to the ground and flash their white rump patches like signal lights saying to all who will look, "I'm a northern harrier."

Another easy-to-identify raptor is the American kestrel,

formerly sparrow hawk, with its black-and-white face pattern and its rufous back and tail. These small falcons, the size of blue jays, slowly lift their tails as they sit on telephone wires watching for grasshoppers, their favorite food. Other than those raptors, though, the ones we see migrating along our ridge can be as confusing as fall warblers since the immatures, again, lack the distinguishing marks of the adults. In such cases, I count on what the English call a bird's "jizz," or general aspect, size, and manner of flying, but I am still a long way from being confident about raptor identification.

Broad-winged hawks, which migrate beginning in late August, are the only raptors that move as a group. They are often so high in the sky that it is hard to see them, and I frequently miss their passing. The first red-tailed and sharp-shinned hawks can also be seen migrating one by one along the ridge top near the end of the month, presaging the hundreds that will pass over during the true autumn season.

Thus August, while primarily a hot summer month, still exhibits "autumnal" signposts—colored leaves, fall wildflowers, food harvesting and storing, migration, and occasional crisp, cool days. And, as the month draws to a close, summer is definitely waning. Shadows are deeper and longer. The resident tufted titmice, white-breasted nuthatches, and black-capped chickadees return from the deep woods with their offspring to reclaim the sovereignty of the yard trees while the visiting songbirds prepare for their long trips south. Once again, I settle back to watch the splendor of an Appalachian autumn.

September

The whole of September and half if not the whole of October, are the finest months in Pennsylvania.

—*Peter Kalm's Travels in North America,*
entry for September 23, 1748

SEPTEMBER 1. It was a day windy and clear enough to see forever, as if autumn blew in overnight, whisking away all the heat and humidity. Migrating warblers were again on the move. Like the birds, I too feel compelled to migrate, yet I also want to stay here, imbued with restless energy and delight in the changing season.

I took a long, leisurely walk down the hollow road this beautiful morning. The upper portion of the stream has been reduced to occasional puddles, but when I checked under rocks for salamanders, I found water oozing up from the steambed. I also discovered two ravine salamanders.

Further down the hollow, below the first of the big hemlock trees, there was a discernible flow of water, and the hollow echoed with sounds of autumn—"cucking" eastern chipmunks, calling blue jays, "yanking" white-breasted nuthatches. In many places, I found eroded dirt trails made by animals coming down to the stream for water.

As I was standing quietly in the road, a raccoon wandered past in the streambed below, lifting rocks, feeling with its fluttery front paws, searching intently for food. It did not see me, so I followed it on the road while it continued upstream for maybe one hundred feet until it did spot my movement. I froze into place as it turned to look me over. What beautiful creatures they are. That one had a bright white-and-black banded tail, mostly white ears, and the usual mask.

Then, downstream, I head a cry, "ooo," owl-like in sound. The raccoon turned around and started back downstream, keeping a wary eye on my motionless form, but becoming less and less concerned by my presence every moment. A little below where I first saw it, another, slightly smaller raccoon was foraging. Its tail was much duller, more dirty gray and white. I assumed it was the remaining offspring of its mother, the larger raccoon, since the young are still traveling and learning from their mothers at this time of year.

They turned over rocks together as I watched, came up on the bank nearest to me to nose in the underbrush, and then went back into the streambed. Each stood up on its haunches like a small bear to look at me, before settling back down to forage in the stream. I could hear quiet communication noises as they worked. Finally, the mother gave a more emphatic grunt and headed up the hill. The youngster followed, a few hundred feet behind and over to the right from its parent, like a small child not altogether willing to do exactly as its parent wants it to do. Eventually, both meandered out of sight.

It is for those moments of enlightenment, those chances to observe the lives of animals, that I go out day after day. I try, when animals do see me, to be totally quiet and nonthreatening, to flood my being with a feeling of affection and regard for them, and those two, at least, seemed to respond by relaxing and continuing on with what they were doing. All the while I watched and they foraged, blue jays screamed above us. Neither raccoons nor I paid them any attention.

SEPTEMBER 2. Our son Steve is the luckiest birdwatcher I know. He merely has to lie abed on a warm afternoon and a rare bird, like Poe's raven, comes tap, tap, tapping at his chamber window.

In reality, the bird landed on a small shrub outside Steve's bedroom window today, and it certainly wasn't a raven. It wasn't even a large bird, but a small, flitty warbler that paused to show off its unusual color pattern— white belly and throat, white wing bars, yellow cap, and a black line through its eye. It was a Brewster's warbler.

Brewster's warbler (*Vermivora "leucobronchialis"*), is a hybrid, the result of mating between a golden-winged warbler and a blue-winged warbler. The mating of those same two species may also produce the less common, recessive type, Lawrence's warbler (*Vermivora "lawrencii"*). The Brewster's looks more like the golden-winged warbler except for its white throat (which is acknowledged in its species name *leucobronchialis,* Greek for "white-throated"), but it has the black line through its eye like the blue-winged warbler. The Lawrence's, on the other hand, has the black mask and throat patch of a golden-winged warbler and the yellow breast of the blue-winged warbler.

Both hybrids may sing like either parent. That means, according to Peterson, "a buzzy beeee-buss (as if inhaled or exhaled)" in the case of a blue-winged warbler or "a buzzy note followed by three on a lower pitch" bee-bz-bz-bz" if the bird is a golden-winged warbler. I have often heard the latter song at the top of First Field during migration, but never that of the former. Yet, apparently, blue-wings have been expanding their range at the expense of golden-wings during the last several decades, probably because golden-wings are choosier about their habitat: they like old fields with a few shrubs or small trees. Blue-wings like this too, but can adapt as the area becomes overgrown with shrubs and trees.

The Brewster's warbler that Steve saw did not sing and was probably not a local bird but a migrant, possibly from Connecticut or Massachusetts where its parents' ranges overlap and where most of the hybridizing takes place. Studies have shown that Brewster's warblers usually do not mate with other hybrids but with either golden- or blue-winged warblers. T. Donald Carter, assistant curator of mammals at the American Museum of Natural History in the mid-twentieth century, watched a banded male Brewster's for six years at his home in Denville, New Jersey. In five of those years, he mated with a female golden-winged warbler.[1]

In May 1986, a pair of Brewster's warblers was found nesting in North Park, Allegheny County, in western Pennsylvania. Luckily, one of the discoverers, Joseph P. Panza, was a photographer and so documented his finding with a colored photo showing two Brewster's warblers feeding nestlings. But there has never been a record of Lawrence's warblers mating with each other or a Brewster's. Kenneth C. Parkes, ornithologist at the Carnegie Museum of Natural History in Pittsburgh, wrote in *Birder's World* that "there appears to be no 'averaging out' of the characters, as we might expect if interbreeding were common between the hybrid and parental warblers." He believes that, "for some reason, the hybrids are at a disadvantage for long-term survival so that the hybrid lines eventually die out."[2]

1. As cited by Terres, *The Audubon Society Encyclopedia of North American Birds*, p. 968.
2. Parkes, "Family Tree," p. 36–37.

Steve called in his discovery to the author of *Birds of Central Pennsylvania,* Merrill Wood, who told him the Brewster's has been reported occasionally over the years for our area, but not the Lawrence's warbler. So while Steve's luck was excellent, it was not perfect. He should have seen a Lawrence's.

SEPTEMBER 3. I took a walk down the hollow this morning. The spicebush berries had already turned a bright red, and I picked one to squeeze and smell its pungent, allspice odor as I walked along. Ferns along the almost-dry streambed were yellowing prematurely because of the drought, and the orange jewelweed, lover of moisture, was sparse.

When Margaret lived in her ancestral home, I never walked over her land, respecting her privacy, but since she moved away I have discovered a whole new area of the mountain and find it wonderful—filled with remote knolls of huge old red oak trees, small hollows overhung with grapevines, and new wildflower species.

Today I discovered that her old driveway was overgrown with white mushrooms sprouting in the tire tracks. The front screen door gaped open; broken tree limbs littered the back lawn. Vegetation engulfed the abandoned, derelict cars and crept into the remains of the shed. Blue jays cried overhead, the only sign of wildlife in the early morning stillness. But as I stood near the old garden, I noticed two huge holes in the ground, the well-used den of some creature—fox, woodchuck, maybe even big enough for a coyote. The creatures were rapidly recolonizing those human-deserted grounds.

Along the Upper Road I found several specimens of Allegheny vine draped over witch hazel trees, the first time I have ever seen this vine on the mountain. Its leaves are like those of the corydalis, and its pinkish white flowers resemble bleeding hearts. Add to that discovery one clump of skunk cabbage (the only clump on the mountain), hundreds of the parasitic squawroots that blanket the ground beneath the oak trees every spring, and Virginia dayflowers growing in a wetland area in the middle of the Lower Road.

Then there are the three side hollows, shaded by large trees with an understory of rattlesnake fern and several species of woodland ferns. Those hollows provide shelter on their southern slopes to a diversity of wildlife, especially birds, during the winter months. It is there, during our Christmas Bird Count, where our sons have made their best discoveries: flocks of wild turkeys; a hermit thrush; eastern bluebirds by the score; large flocks of American robins; even, once, a golden eagle flying over. How much more is there to discover here in this unique section of the hollow, and how much time do I have?

Lying with my head in the crotch of a split tree along the first side hollow, legs stretched out comfortably, I spotted a fox squirrel harvesting a hickory nut from a small tree nearby. It spotted me too and climbed cautiously out on a limb to feed in full view. Fox squirrels have been quietly colonizing the mountain, seemingly able to live in harmony with the more abundant gray squirrels. Slower moving, with a more placid disposition, they are the epitome of "watchable wildlife." And so I watched. Alternatively eating and scolding me in a quiet undertone, it finished the nut before climbing back down the tree and disappearing.

Because I was tired, I meandered slowly along, stopping often, sitting, lying down, less hurried and more open than usual. This receptive mood seems to be the one that nature responds to most readily, when I do not try to see how much territory I can cover but merely receive what nature has to offer. As is usual with me, though, when I walk over this property, I headed into the heart of the hollow, what I call the "wilderness grove," a knoll of old-growth red oak trees where I can sit and hear no human-induced noises and see nothing but trees and un-inhabited mountainside wherever I look.

No one was there; no one will likely be there until hunting season. Wood pewees called their drawn out "pee-a-wees," eastern chipmunks "cuck-cucked," a ruffed grouse exploded from the underbrush. It was difficult to believe that less than a mile away in either direction there were highways, farms, several villages, a town, and the main east-west railroad line; in fact, according to the U.S. Census Bureau, we live in an SMSA, a Standard Metro-politan Statistical Area.

SEPTEMBER 4. Nothing is more alluring on a clear, blue, September day than a patch of goldenrod. There, where life is never static, I can watch the last frenzy of the insect world—beetles mating, bees and wasps gathering pollen and nectar, and butterflies feeding.

We have let most of our thirty-seven-acre First Field, formerly a hayfield, "go to weeds," as one neighbor was overheard saying. Bruce cuts a small swatch every year, enough to keep the black locust trees at the edge of the field where they belong, but I am out watching him like a hawk. "Don't cut the goldenrod," I beg, as he bounces along on his tractor. "Watch out for the wild roses." "Go easy on the blackberries." "Oh no, you've mowed down a black raspberry bush." How can any self-respecting, part-time countryman keep a hayfield in shape when he has a naturalist for a wife?

We have five species of goldenrod in our field—the red-stemmed, sharp-leaved or cut-leaved goldenrod (*Solidago arguta*), rough-stemmed goldenrod (*S. rugosa*), the sweetly scented, lance-leaved goldenrod (*S. graminifolia*), and tall goldenrod (*S. altissima*). The fifth species, Canada goldenrod (*S. canadensis*), is distinguished by roundish stem swellings called goldenrod ball galls that are made by a member of the fly family, *Eurosta solidaginis*.

After mating in May, the females deposit an egg on the growing Canada goldenrod plant. The larva secretes a liquid that alters the genetics of the affected area, causing a ball-shaped swelling which serves as a home for the growing insect. I have sliced the ball gall open in late summer and found a plump, cream-colored maggot inside. Had I not disturbed it, that maggot would have over-wintered in the gall and emerged as an adult the following spring.

All goldenrod species are attractive to insects. According to the entomologist John Henry Comstock, in his classic *Manual for the Study of Insects,* "To the enthusiastic entomologist the goldenrod is a rich mine, yielding to the collector more treasures than any other flower" (pp. 570–71). A nature-watcher like me also mines goldenrod for vignettes of insect behavior. But of all the goldenrod species I have observed, the tall goldenrod, sporting thick, bright yellow plumes, provides the greatest entertainment.

One day I counted eight honeybees, a bumblebee, a carpenter bee, and two mating pairs—locust borers and soldier beetles—on a single plume. Multiply that kind of activity in a patch of several hundred plants and the insect life seems overwhelming.

This afternoon I spent the better part of two hours meandering through the goldenrod. Two kinds of sulphur butterflies, the orange (*Colias eurytheme*) and the white cabbage (*Pieris rapae*), fluttered from flower to flower or whirled above the patch in dizzying combat. The larger, slower flying monarch butterflies occasionally landed on a plume to feed before continuing on their southward migration to the mountains of Mexico. Another striking species of butterfly, the great-spangled fritillary (*Speyeria cybele*), whose larvae fed on violets back in the spring, also supped from goldenrod blossoms.

Except for the white cabbage, orange seemed to be the predominant color of the butterflies that frequented the goldenrod. It was also the color of one of the several beetle species I found there, the handsome Pennsylvania soldier beetle (*Chauliognathus pennsylvanicus*). Like the monarch and orange sulphur butterflies, black was its accent color, and, like the bees, it also fed on both the nectar and pollen of the flowers.

Spider webs were strung from plant to plant as traps for the unwary. One web I found held the bound, mummified body of an incautious honeybee, set aside by a spider already satiated with the juices of other victims. Most web-weaving spiders can go months without a good meal, and the patience of a spider, as it hangs motionless, upside down, in the middle of its web, waiting for a meal, is legendary. I was stopped for a time by *Argiope riparia,* one of the largest and most conspicuous of the round-web spiders. That black and yellow species was an inch long, with front legs larger than her body. I knew it was a female because they are larger than the males, and only the females of that species spin the distinctive webs.

These webs have a thick, zigzag band of white silk up and down across the middle and a circular area where the spider waits. They make no nests and so they always hang in the middle of their webs waiting. In September they lay their eggs in large, pear-shaped cocoons which are hung among grasses and bushes by threads. The young hatch in the winter and stay in their cocoons until May, when they emerge as spiderlings. By the first of August they are mature, ready to mate and begin the cycle anew.

That particular *A. riparia* (most spiders do not have common names) had a number of small corpses festooning her web. She never moved while I watched, and no insect blundered near. After half an hour, I left what Walt Whitman referred to as a "noiseless, patient spider" and wandered on through the field.

My attention was caught by the abundance of colorful, red-legged, black and yellow locust borers. There seemed to be several on every goldenrod plant I examined. These beautiful but destructive beetles (*Megacyllene robinae*) are harmful in their larval stage to black locust trees. The females deposit their eggs in the rough crevices of black locust bark from late August until the middle of October. The eggs hatch in a week and the larvae bore into the inner bark where they winter in a dormant state. Early in the spring they tunnel into the woody portion of the trees, which weakens the locusts, and the larvae use the borings to plug the outer end of their pupal cells. They pupate and emerge as adults in August or early September and then fly to their food source—goldenrod—to find mates.

I watched two locust borers mating on the topmost branch of a goldenrod plant. From below, another borer came bustling up. He approached the pair head-on, using his antennae to sniff the female for odorous signs of her mating readiness. The mating male withdrew and started a fierce tumbling battle with the intruder while the female moved out of the opponents' range. The males fought for a few seconds, and then one fell to the weeds below. The victor immediately claimed the female, but she would have none of him. She struggled and ran over the blossoms, and, as I bent closer, I could hear the faintest of squeaks. Finally that male flew off.

I assumed that the victor in the battle had been the intruder and that, for some reason known only to the female locust borer, she had not found him appealing. At least, that was how it appeared to my anthropomorphic eyes.

Would anyone have believed that female locust borers could be choosey?

Just imagine, if Bruce had insisted on keeping a perfect hayfield, I would have missed the courtship of a female locust borer.

SEPTEMBER 5. Our hearts are heavy. A friend of ours, acting as our straw man, has been trying to buy the adjoining 100-acre property from the lumberman owner who plans to log it. We have offered him all of our life savings, which was not enough. He told our friend that he had almost closed a deal with two lumbermen from another city for nearly double his purchase price. If that falls through, he will cut the forest himself because he believes that "those trees have to come off." Only after the cutting would our friend's offer be a fair price for the land.

If it weren't so beautiful here, I would have advocated selling and moving away long ago. It has been so difficult, year after year, to live with this uncertainty about the hollow and the safety of our access road, but, most of all, the almost certain knowledge that in the end we will probably lose and the lumberman will have his way. Will he do a careful, selective cut as he promised and stay those crucial 200 feet above the road?

The specter of a clear-cut in the hollow continues to haunt me. From everything I can read about it, clear-cutting does violence to the entire web of forest life. Because it promotes compaction of the surface soil, it exposes the forest floor to intense drying and evaporation. This either destroys or greatly alters the normal hospitality of the soil to fungi, bacteria, worms, and microscopic plants and animals of all kinds which are necessary to reproduce the cutover forest in some semblance of its former self. Instead, the flora and fauna are completely changed, and only the "generalists," those plants and animals that can live almost anywhere, recolonize a clear-cut. Already, in greatly disturbed areas such as the powerline right-of-way and where the lumberman built new roads, hay-scented ferns have moved in. They produce chemicals that inhibit the root growth of other plants, including tree seedlings. That same drying-out effect increases the danger of fire, and because our only way out is down the hollow, a fire sweeping up it would trap us.

Clear-cutting nearly always implies the use of the heaviest machinery, which also creates havoc among all the lesser creatures and plants. One study indicates that most of the amphibian population was crushed in clear-cut areas. Gordon Robinson, a forest researcher, claims that the "oversized and unwieldly equipment used by logging operators is totally unacceptable" in any case and that most "American foresters notoriously disregard the effects of logging practices upon soils."[3] Another study, by Duffy and Meier, has shown that the recovery of herbaceous understory plants of eastern deciduous forests from a clear-cut may take centuries, rather than only decades as biologists once thought.

Furthermore, clear-cutting causes erosion, especially on steep slopes with thin soil and a southern exposure such as that on our neighbor's land. This could lead to the silting of our clear-flowing stream.

Another concern to us is the possibility of landslides onto our road. Cutting across a mountainside and bulldozing roads moves tons of dirt, destabilizing slopes and leading to landslides. Even more alarming is that landslide danger *increases* five to twenty years after clear-cutting because part of the strength of a soil mass comes from the

3. Robinson, "The Sierra Club Position on Clear-Cutting and Forest Management," p. 16.

anchoring effect of tree roots which take that long to decay after the initial logging. We have already contended with small landslides due to the inherent instability of our mountainside. To be faced with larger landslides when we are seventy years old is a frightening prospect.

To escape my worry over the hollow, I headed up to Laurel Ridge. Dozens of chimney swifts were twittering back and forth over the powerline right-of-way just as they were the evening of Labor Day. I don't remember seeing such numbers here before. And while it was clear and sunny on the mountaintop, the valley below billowed with thick fog—a typical fall phenomenon. Not only the sky above the right-of-way, but the sky over Laurel Ridge Trail teemed with chimney swifts, coursing back and fourth in search of insects, chittering to let me know they were there. I imagined them joining streams of chimney swifts heading for Peru in long, undulating columns, weaving their way, like plumes of smoke, southward for the winter. Have I somehow missed this chimney swift migration over the mountain during the twenty autumns I have lived here? Or have they shifted their migration route?

Along the Far Field Trail I stopped to watch a bold eastern box turtle. He swelled his yellow throat in and out like a child who keeps trying to blow up a balloon but is unsuccessful. Although I stood less than four feet away he did not characteristically retreat into his shell. But then I often find box turtles behaving strangely in autumn, almost as if they are enjoying the last of the warmth before burrowing into the ground for the winter.

SEPTEMBER 6. Today is the perfect day to observe some of the woodland wildflowers along our hollow road and the relationship between their flowers and the pollinating insects. Take, for instance, the bright yellow, smooth false foxglove (*Gerardia laevigata*) that sprawls over the banks. This member of the snapdragon family has deep, tubelike flowers which only the long tongues of bumblebees can reach into to secure nectar. But how the bumblebee does this is a surprise.

At first I thought, as I watched the foxglove, that the bumblebee I was observing was unusual. It would land on the edge of a flower, turn over on its back, and wriggle upside down deep into the blossom. Then other bumblebees came along and did the same thing. Later, when I checked my library, I read that because of the shape of the flower, the upside-down approach is the only way the bumblebees can reach the nectar.

How, though, does the bumblebee pollinate the flower? When the bee turns upside down, the male, pollen-bearing anthers hang above its belly and brush it with pollen. Then the bee proceeds to the next blossom. The female stigma sticks out beyond the flower so that the bee leaves pollen dust on it before it turns upside down.

As I was watching the foxgloves, I suddenly heard the buzz of a ruby-throated hummingbird. To my surprise, it began sucking nectar from the rather insignificant pale yellow blossoms of the weedy-looking horse-balm (*Collinsonia canadensis*) across the road. This member of the mint family has strongly lemon-scented flowers that smell just like the cultivated herb lemon balm. In addition to furnishing nectar for the hummingbird, it was also popular with bumblebees and honeybees. Because the male and female parts of horse-balm protrude a good half-inch beyond the blossom, it is a flower that can be pollinated by many nectar-loving insects.

Keeping company with the horse-balm were the pink-tinted white blossoms of turtlehead (*Chelone glabra*). Another member of the snapdragon family, it can only be pollinated by the largest of bumblebees. Its completely enclosed flower opens to the pushing and prying of a bumblebee on its lower lip when the anthers are laden with pollen. The pollen is thick and woolly, and the four kidney-shaped, translucent anthers hang above the lower lip so the bumblebee's back is brushed with pollen as it pushes its way down into the blossom in pursuit of nectar.

It backs out of the flower, again brushing the anthers, and continues on to other flowers. Since the female stigma, which is also located above the lower lip of the flower, only matures after the anthers wither, the bumble-bee does its pollinating by going from younger, pollen-bearing blossoms to older stigma-matured flowers.

Further down the hollow I watched still another flower pollination drama, this time on the orange jewelweed or touch-me-nots (*Impatiens capensis*). I had read that they are primarily bird flowers and that ruby-throated hummingbirds are their chief pollinators. But as I sat observing the plants, I heard the steady buzzing of honeybees. I looked more closely and saw that the honeybees approached the backs of the blossoms, which had semicircular small tubes containing the nectar. The honeybees would grasp the slender tubes with their forefeet, pierce them with their probiscises, and suck out the nectar without pollinating the flowers. The Italian honeybees, which most beekeepers prefer, evolved in harmony with European, not North American wildflowers, which may be why they "steal" the nectar.

North American-evolved bumblebees, on the other hand, did as they were supposed to. They wriggled deep into the blossoms, brushing against a bunch of united anthers that hung over the entrance. Those anthers were loaded with a white pollen that covered the backs of the bumblebees, annoying them so much that after visiting only one or two blossoms, they would invariably land on a sapling growing in the midst of the touch-me-not patch, cling to a branch with their forelegs, and thoroughly clean off their backs. I never did see a hummingbird on the flowers, but the touch-me-nots have hedged their bets. They also have cleistogamous blossoms whose function is not to bloom but to ripen self-fertilized seeds.

So each wildflower has its own devices, despite occasional thieves like the honeybees, for ensuring the continuation of the species, and by watching carefully, I learn more about the ways of wildflowers and pollinating insects.

SEPTEMBER 7. The leaves are coloring fast and early, probably because of the continuing drought. The black gums are now red and orange, the black birches bright yellow, and the blueberry shrubs reddish purple. But for nearly a decade, what looks like autumn color comes as early as July. That is when all the black locust trees turn a reddish brown from the infestation of locust leaf miners (*Odonata dorsalis*). Since the late 1800s they have been recognized as a pest species in Pennsylvania.

I first noticed a browning of the leaves in some of the locust trees along the base of Sapsucker Ridge nine summers ago. The next summer more trees were attacked. The following year the leaf miners reached the trees in our front yard, and since then every tree, young or old, is infested. The browning is caused by the larvae of these attractive, quarter-inch-long, orange and black beetles. Adults winter over in protected places, under fallen leaves for instance, and emerge, in Pennsylvania, during late April to mid-May when black locust leaves, the last to appear, are unfolding. They feed on black locust foliage as well as that of apple, crabapple, oak, and other trees. They mate on host trees, and the females lay clusters of three to five overlapping eggs on the surface of the locust leaves. Then they cover the eggs with excrement so that they cannot be seen by possible predators.

In a little over a week the eggs begin hatching. Every clump of eggs works as a team; the first larva to hatch makes a hole in the leaf and the other larvae follow it to live for two to four days in the same "mine." Like all leaf-mining insects (and there are great numbers of them in four separate insect orders), they eat the green material called mesophyll between the upper and lower skin of a leaf. This digging out of the valuable green part of the leaf from between the "skin" layers reminded entomologists of coal miners retrieving a seam of coal from between two worthless strata—hence the name "leaf miners."

While many leaf-mining larvae confine their damage to the one leaf they enter after hatching, locust leaf miners soon leave their communal leaf, each moving to a separate leaf. Over their approximately eighteen-day development they keep going from leaf to leaf, damaging each one they enter. Each larva uses three to four leaflets during its larval stage until it pupates in the last "mine" it has dug out.

Finally, seven to ten days later, the adult beetle breaks through the epidermis of the leaf and spends the rest of the summer skeletonizing the lower surface of the leaves and eating small, oblong holes in them. But the damage they do is minor compared to that done in their larval stage. By late September, most adult beetles are already hibernating.

Since locust leaf miners are a native species, other insects have adapted to feed on them and other pests. One predator, the so-called wheel bug (*Arilus cristatus*), pierces the leaf miner larva with its sharp beak directly through the leaf's epidermis and injects a powerful venom which digests and liquifies the inner tissues of the prey. This material is then pumped into the wheel bug's stomach through a hollow duct in its beak. They also attack adult beetles.

But apparently Pennsylvania does not have enough wheel bugs; every year the trees look worse, not only on our mountain but throughout the state. Although these infestations do not kill the trees, they do weaken them, making them more susceptible to disease and to attacks by the more lethal locust borers. Not long ago I asked a forester why no one seems upset about the damage in contrast to the mass hysteria that erupts whenever there is a gypsy moth caterpillar outbreak. He told me that black locusts are not important landscape trees nor are they useful to the lumbering industry, so they are allowed to live out their life cycles unmolested and unregarded by humans, while the gypsy moth caterpillars destroy trees considered valuable by the timber industry.

SEPTEMBER 8. Every autumn at this time I look for flowers that I discovered growing through the thick layer of moss on the Guesthouse Trail seven years ago. They looked like red and gold Indian pipes, except that instead of one pipe to a stem, there were several. I counted sixty-three individual plants in that one patch. But although I searched through the rest of the woods, I did not find another colony. Where had they come from?

Later, I consulted my field guides and identified them as pinesaps (*Monotropa hypopitys*). As I suspected, they were closely related to the Indian pipes (*Monotropa uniflora*) of midsummer's dark woods. Some botanists have classified them in a single family—*Monotropaceae*—while others place them in *Pyrolaceae* with pipsissewa and pyrola.

Monotropa is Greek for "having a single turn." The name is appropriate because the top of the stem of pinesaps and Indian pipes is turned to one side, causing the pipes to nod. The *uniflora* of Indian pipes means "one flower," referring to the single pipe while the *hypopitys* of pinesaps is translated as "under a pine or fir." Its preferred habitat is in northern Europe where the forests are mostly coniferous. Indian pipes, too, are not unique to North America and can be found in eastern Asia as well. Once they are pollinated, the pipes of both pinesaps and Indian pipes turn skyward and the plants blacken.

Because they lack chlorophyll, both flowers had once been considered parasitic plants. They were thoroughly maligned by Neltje Blanchan in her 1916 *Wild Flowers* volume for the New Nature Library. She called them "degenerates" and claimed that "among their race [they were] branded with the mark of crime as surely as was Cain" because they "live by piracy, to drain the already digested food of [their] neighbors" (pp. 233–34). Such purple prose, while entertaining, later proved inaccurate when botanists upgraded both species to saprophytes. Instead of sapping nutrients from living plants, as parasites do, saprophytes live on dead or decaying matter.

Then Erik Björkman of the Royal School of Forestry in Stockholm, Sweden, noticed that the same fungus completely encloses the roots of both Indian pipes and pinesaps. Their seeds will germinate, but not grow until the fungus is on their roots. Björkman decided to find out if there was any connection between pinesap roots and those of the trees. He put cylinders of sheet metal around clumps of pinesaps which he pounded deep into the earth, severing their roots from those of the neighboring trees.

The following year the isolated pinesaps had very weak growth, compared to the vigorous growth of those that had not been disturbed. Then Björkman injected the nearby spruce and pine trees with glucose containing radioactive carbon 14 as a tracer. Five days later the stems of the undisturbed pinesaps also had radioactive glucose. Further experiments proved that the roots of pinesaps and nearby tree roots are not directly connected, but that the fungus is a nutrient bridge over which carbohydrates in the trees travel to pinesaps. Other nutrients, like phosphorous, use the same bridge to travel from pinesaps to tree roots. So Björkman now calls pinesaps and their relative Indian pipes "epiparasites" on trees. Other botanists say they are probably symbiotic plants—plants that give as well as receive food from other plants.

None of this answers the question, though, as to why pinesaps suddenly appeared on our trail seven years ago, produced only a few plants the following year, and have not been seen since, there or any other place on the mountain. But every year I look hopefully. What was once resurrected for a couple autumns may be resurrected again.

SEPTEMBER 9. The acorns are abundant this year. Along the Laurel Ridge Trail, I stopped to watch a pair of gray squirrels gather them. One scolded and flicked its tail at me as I stood silently watching and then clicked my tongue in answer. Finally, it relaxed and sat ten feet away in the low crotch of a small chestnut oak, chewing on an acorn and keeping one eye on me. Whenever I moved slightly, it stopped chewing and watched until I clicked reassuringly at it. Then it went back to eating. But when I tried to ease myself into a sitting position, it zipped across to a larger tree and disappeared behind the trunk.

Hidden back in the woods, a part of the sun and shadows, I glimpsed, near the ground, what looked like an ear. With the binoculars, I picked out a doe sitting and watching me, her ears pricked up, and I wondered how often I am watched by wild creatures I never see.

I, in turn, sometimes watch creatures that do not see me. As I sat at the top of First Field, a six-point buck crossed below, closely followed by a doe. When he turned around, she feinted with her front legs. Then she danced in front of him for a second or two before running back in the direction she had come from. He looked after her as if bemused and then bent down to graze. Had I seen preliminary courtship rites with female as seductress, male as indifferent? During the rut in November, the tables are turned with male as pursuer, female as indifferent.

The view from the top of First Field was crystal clear to the farthest ridges, and I sat there for hours with the wind blowing through the grasses, the trees billowing like waves on the ridge above. I felt the limitless roll of the ocean rocking me in rhythm with the spinning earth, the sky cloudless, a single turkey vulture soaring past, tilting literally, as I was figuratively, with the wind.

SEPTEMBER 10. This is the time of year when almost everyone begins to see woolly bear caterpillars. I saw my first one yesterday in the hollow. Although some sages even try to foretell the coming winter weather by the width of the black and brown bands encircling the caterpillar's fat body, I am content to record their seasonal appearance. In this case, the caterpillar had a large band of black in front and a small tip of black at the other end with a broad brown band in the middle. But while woolly bears, those larvae of the *Isia isabella* moths, are especially attractive creatures, there are also many other interesting butterfly and moth larvae crawling about.

Caterpillars are the second, or larval, stage in the four stages of moths' and butterflies' lives. First, the eggs are laid and from them hatch the myriad of caterpillars that enjoy chomping everything green from oak leaves to parsley. After increasing their size through several molts, or skin sheddings, the caterpillars change into their pupal, or resting, forms, sometimes for just a week or two like the monarch butterfly. More commonly, though, pupal cases become secure overwintering homes, as is the case for cecropia moths and black swallowtail butterflies.

I have been catching, identifying, and raising caterpillars for the last several weeks. An array of Mason jars on our bow window shelf holds a number of interesting pupae. I found the first specimen munching on my parsley back in late August, and despite its food tastes I had to admire its bright green body with bands of gold-dotted black. Carefully, I picked the parsley stem and carried it and the caterpillar back to the house where I stuffed it into a jar with a perforated top. I easily identified my find as a black swallowtail (*Papilio polyxenes*) butterfly larva. It had hatched from yellowish, ovoid eggs laid on the undersides of some member of the wild or domesticated carrot family, in this case parsley, although parsnips, celery, and carrots themselves are also popular black swallowtail caterpillar food. The caterpillar I had picked up was mature, and after a couple of days it spun its small, dark gray cocoon. I am hoping it will emerge next spring as it is supposed to.

In contrast to that ordinary-sized caterpillar, I found on the first of September a real monster that was sluggishly stretched out on the road beneath a small, wild black cherry tree. Over three inches long with a blimplike shape, it was lime green in color. A series of red knobs covered its head end, and down the middle of its back were two rows of yellow spines flanked on either side by a row of blue spines. It grasped the cherry stem I gave it with eight suckered feet and ate cherry leaves for several days before attaching its large brown cocoon lengthwise to a cherry stem. This caterpillar was the larva of a cecropia moth (*Hyalophora cecropia*), and it too is now settled in for the winter.

Not so the monarch butterfly caterpillar I found on a milkweed plant back on August 26. It was striped white, black, and yellow, and the day after I put it in a jar, it climbed up to the lid and pupated. A butterfly pupa is often called a chrysalis, which means "pertaining to gold," and the monarch butterfly's chrysalis is a good example of this. A shiny green elongated sphere, it has six gold spots in a semicircle at its base and gold lines radiating from its top, quite a contrast to the dully colored pupae of the black swallowtail and the cecropia.

Every day I have watched for the great change, but the chrysalis hung quiescent. Then today, the one day I had to be away, I came home to find a monarch butterfly in my jar. Since it was evening, I put the butterfly on my hanging planter and watched as it slowly ascended one of the macramé ropes, all the while pumping its wings to their proper size and magnificence.

SEPTEMBER 11. This morning the monarch butterfly climbed onto my proffered forefinger and wrapped its legs around it while I carried it outside to a milkweed plant. I had to carefully pry its legs loose and place it on the plant where I left it. Although I had missed its metamorphosis, I still felt privileged to have played a small part in the drama that changed a chrysalis into a butterfly.

As I started out on my morning walk, wave after wave of common grackles flew up the hollow and surged over the Guesthouse Trail. When they took off in a whirl it sounded like a strong gust of wind. They foraged as they moved among the tree leaves, and I saw one pick up a caterpillar and eat it. From the powerline right-of-way, I watched them flow, rank after rank, along First Field.

Then, as I walked along the Far Field Road, I discovered them in the trees, the understory, and on the ground, searching for food. One had a long caterpillar hanging out of its beak. Another flew up with a katydid. The woods and road ahead of me shimmered with iridescent purple bodies set off by bright yellow eyes. The air around me rustled and fluttered. I was surrounded by chuckling grackles. Some flew so close that I could hear the whistle of their wings. The spectacle kept moving, like a river of water, for at least ten minutes before the woods were silent again. A gaggle of grackles is a fine sight to me even though they are generally disliked by most people.

This dislike, I discovered, dates back to at least the mid–eighteenth century when, according to Peter Kalm, Linnaeus's emissary to North America, grackles were known as "purple corn thieves." "They come," he wrote, "in great swarms in spring, soon after the corn is planted. They snatch up the kernels of corn and eat them. As soon as the leaf comes up, they take hold of it with their bills, and pull it up, together with the corn or grain; and thus they give a great deal of trouble to the country people, even so early in spring." Once the corn was ripe, he reported, "they assemble by thousands in the corn fields and exact a heavy tax. . . . They fly in incredibly large flocks in autumn; and it can hardly be conceived whence such immense numbers of them can come. When they rise in the air they darken the sky, and make it look almost black. They are then in such great numbers and so close together that it is surprising how they find room to move their wings."

Then people decided to get rid of them by putting a price on their heads. Pennsylvania and New Jersey paid threepence a dozen for dead grackles. New England nearly extirpated them. "But in the summer of the year 1749 an immense quantity of worms appeared on the meadows, which devoured the grass, and did great damage, so the people repented of their enmity against the corn thieves for they thought they had observed that those birds lived chiefly on such worms before the corn was ripe, and consequently exterminated them, or at least prevented their increasing too much. . . . But after these enemies and destroyers of the worms were killed off, the worms were of course more at liberty to multiply, and therefore they grew so numerous that they did more mischief now than the birds did before."[4] Evidently, we have not changed much over the last two-and-a-half centuries. Many people still believe there are simplistic solutions to what we perceive as "pest" problems.

SEPTEMBER 12. At this time of year I can find deer in three different coats—the reddish brown of summer, the gray of winter, and the brown and gray of change. Each deer seems to change at its own pace, and I find chunks of shed hair along the trails. This morning three does fed in the yard, one in her gray winter coat and another in her brown summer coat. The third doe was mostly brown with graying the length of her backbone. Why do deer change their coats on different schedules?

Later, I surprised two magnificent eight-point bucks feeding together on Laurel Ridge. They did not notice me for a minute or two as I stood less than one hundred feet from them. Then one buck suddenly looked up, stared in my direction, and snorted. Both fled in an instant. Bucks are always more alert than does, more intimidating in their stance, disappearing with less fuss and noise and much faster than hesitant does that blunder, snort several times, pause, look back, and make a general, bumbling hullabaloo before fading from view. So, merely by its actions, I can distinguish a buck from a doe. I don't need to see antlers.

SEPTEMBER 13. As I walked down the hollow road, I approached within twenty feet of a grazing doe. She looked and stamped and finally resumed eating pokeberries and striped maple leaves. Then I heard a rustling noise behind

4. Kalm, *Travels in North America*, pp. 249–50.

me and turned slowly around, coming almost face-to-face with a fox squirrel ten feet away in a witch hazel tree. As usual with those phlegmatic squirrels, it went about its business while I lay down on the ground to watch it. The squirrel proceeded to climb up several more small witch hazel trees and pick the green fruits which it then stripped open to get at the kernel.

Witch hazels are not much more than shrubs, something the fox squirrel seemed to know instinctively because it spread its body evenly over several limbs that bent beneath its weight as it ate dozens of witch hazel nuts. Once it climbed down to rumble at me, switching its red and gray tail up and down. Like other fox squirrels I have observed, this one seemed to be the epitome of dignity because it moved slower and more carefully than the derring-do gray squirrels. Instead of bravado leaps, it crawled cautiously over the limbs. After half an hour, it hopped slowly off.

Later, back at home, I watched a gray squirrel tumble thirty feet to the ground from a branch on the black walnut in the driveway. It seemed none the worse for its fall because it immediately jumped up and scampered off.

SEPTEMBER 14. A beautiful day here on the mountaintop, but there was the usual autumn fog in the valley. From the powerline right-of-way the scene was like a Chinese painting, the valley filled with billowing clouds and only the blue tops of the distant ridges showing.

Pileated, downy, and hairy woodpeckers worked the tree trunks on Laurel Ridge Trail. One common yellowthroat sang its "witchedy, witchedy" song. An ovenbird skulked through the underbrush, keeping an alert eye on me. Eastern chipmunks scrambled about in search of acorns. I could still hear the calls of eastern wood pewees and rufous-sided towhees, American robins and American goldfinches, red-eyed vireos and blue jays.

Blue jays, in fact, announced my presence as I sat quietly at the base of a tree atop Sapsucker Ridge, but at first the flock of birds nearby paid them no heed. Then the tufted titmice decided to protest my presence. One even landed on a sapling six feet away and scolded loudly, a metaphorical sneer on its face. Then it flipped to eight feet away and scolded again. There were answering scolds further off, but in less than a minute, as I sat unmoving, they went off to join the unflappable, foraging black-capped chickadees. They had done their duty.

SEPTEMBER 15. The unsightly webs that bizarrely festoon many hardwood trees in late summer and early autumn are woven by fall webworms (*Hyphantria cunea*). They are the offspring of small white moths which overwinter as lacy, brown-colored cocoons in the soil.

Once they hatch in May they mate and then lay clusters of eggs on the undersides of tree leaves. The eggs hatch into hairy, grayish caterpillars with shiny, reddish brown heads, a series of double black dots on their backs, and red brown dots along their sides. They immediately migrate to the tip end of the tree branches where they spin their webs to protect themselves as they skeletonize the leaves of the trees.

In Pennsylvania there are usually two broods of fall webworms. The first, in late June, is not particularly noticeable because its numbers are low. But during bad years, which occur every seven to ten years, the late brood, in August and early September, disfigures the landscape. Scientists do not know why heavy outbreaks occur, but it probably has something to do with weather conditions.

Fall webworms will eat the leaves of any hardwood tree, although they do have definite preferences. Here on the mountain they choose only black walnut, wild black cherry, and our one crabapple sapling. The damage they do is minimal, however, because the leaves have already completed most of their cycle and will soon be discarded by the trees anyway.

Yesterday I stopped to watch the caterpillars working on a cherry sapling beside the trail. The tree was six feet high and contained three small nests, but the rest of the sapling was veiled in long strands of silk. The silk was extremely sticky, and when I touched it, it clung to my fingers more firmly than a spider's web.

Next, I took a large stick and poked it into the silk that surrounded one nest. It adhered to the stick like cotton candy, and I held aloft a nest of wriggling caterpillars which I dropped on the ground across the path from the cherry tree. I also removed the second nest and put it in the middle of the trail, while the third I left in the tree. There seemed to be no immediate reaction to my meddling; knowing how slowly but inexorably insects work, I waited until today to note any changes.

I found that the nest on the trail was almost empty of worms. I also noticed several caterpillars crawling back to the sapling to resume eating, so I assumed they had all returned to the home tree. However, the second nest was bustling with activity. New silk lines had been sent out in several directions, but they only encased grass blades. Since fall webworms do not eat grass, they will all be dead in a few days, unable to cope constructively with my tampering.

I had a good look at a larger fall webworm nest that had blown down from a taller tree. With my hand lens, I examined several of the caterpillars and found one with a cluster of eggs near its head. Some of the eggs were hatching, and the caterpillar was twitching violently since it was being eaten alive by the offspring of a parasitic fly. Nature is often not nice, not even to insects which, at this time of year, always seem almost certain to inherit the earth, so prolific are they. But for every native pest, there are usually native controls as well. Those webworms that escape parasites, though, will soon reach their full, one-inch length. Then they will crawl down the trees and into the soil to pupate for the winter. But their nests, filled with their droppings and dried-leaf bits, will remain as souvenirs of their activity until the winter winds scour most of them from the tree branches.

SEPTEMBER 16. Storm after storm rolled over the mountain today, beginning before dawn and continuing long after dark, keeping me housebound for the first time in many months this droughty year. One fierce storm late in the afternoon had high winds and rain so heavy I couldn't see beyond the driveway. Hailstones pounded against the windows. Finally, I took refuge in the basement at the height of the wind, which brought down the old apple tree in the grape tangle. Thunder and lightning were almost simultaneous, but it was the wind I hid from. Ten years ago, while we were away, a miniature tornado touched down in the hollow and cleared a swath of trees up the mountainside, so whenever the winds blow hard, I head for the basement.

Near sunset, though, one of the storms produced a double rainbow. A pileated woodpecker stripped bark from a treetop just below the end of the rainbow, unaware that he should have been looking for a pot of gold instead, while an eastern phoebe, undeterred by the rain, kept sallying off the topmost limb of the old dead oak to catch insects.

The sunlight shining through the falling rain cast a shining, purple glow over the pokeberries, which made them gleam like crusted jewels standing out against the richness of the goldenrod bent down next to the berries. Those two manifestations of royalty and wealth—purple and gold—were all the riches I wanted or needed.

SEPTEMBER 17. Five years ago, during a hollow walk, I made a momentous discovery. After searching for years beneath the enormous American beech trees that grow along our stream, I finally found what I was looking for beneath the spindly, beech saplings sprouting from the road bank above: beechdrops, those parasitic wildflowers that get their nutrients from the roots of beech trees. Once again I wondered, as I had about their close relatives the pinesaps, had I missed them all the previous autumns or had they appeared that year for the first time?

All I know is that I have easily found beechdrops every autumn since then, although some years there are more than others. Beechdrops (*Epifagus virginiana*) are members of the Broomrape family and, like other parasitic flowers, lack green pigment. Fleshy tan in color, they blend in well with the understory so if you don't know what you are looking at, you might mistake them for tree sprouts, especially after they bloom and dry up for the year. In fact, evidence of beechdrops is easier to see in winter when there is no competition from more exuberant, short-lived understory plants. Beechdrops, like jewelweeds, violets, and wood sorrel, among others, have both cleistogamous flowers which never open but produce many seeds, and small purplish striped flowers above them which are sterile.

Today I took a hollow walk, and after only a little searching I found beechdrops blooming on both the bank above the road and the slope below. They were not as abundant as they have been in past years, but that may be because of the drought, which has already affected the abundance of the midsummer parasitic Indian pipes.

At dusk Bruce and I sat out on the veranda, listening to the silence until we suddenly heard from the top of First Field what sounded like a bobwhite call. Six times it repeated a clearly whistled "bob-white!" What else could it be but the northern bobwhite? But this is the first time we have ever heard one in our twenty years here.

SEPTEMBER 18. Bruce again heard five bobwhite calls coming from the top of First Field at 6:15 this morning, so I was up poking along the woods edges searching for them an hour later. I found one vocal gray catbird, calling blue jays, rufous-sided towhees and Carolina wrens, and one scolding house wren, but not a trace of a northern bobwhite. I called my friend and local bird expert, Dave, and he told me that there are often bobwhite escapees from the game farm in the valley below. But wherever the bird had come from, it became the one hundred and sixty-third species for our mountain.

Noise from blue jays and northern flickers brought me out into the yard in time to see a pileated woodpecker chasing a Cooper's hawk out of a black walnut tree near the shed and up into the front yard. The birds continued to harry it so it flew over the house to a black locust tree and then finally circled high into the sky, joining the stream of raptors migrating along the ridgetop today.

Steve first announced the migration when he climbed up on the guesthouse roof to rebuild the chimney that had blown over in the March winds several springs ago. After only a few minutes up there with Bruce, he came running into the main house to get his binoculars, a pencil, and notebook. From 10:00 A.M. until 5:00 P.M. with an hour off for lunch, he recorded seven sharp-shinned hawks, eighteen turkey vultures, twenty-seven red-tailed hawks, three American kestrels, one unidentified accipiter, five ospreys and ninety broad-winged hawks.

The last two species were the most exciting. Two of the ospreys had hovered over the guesthouse, giving Bruce and Steve a close-up look at this striking bird of prey. Ospreys are no longer as scarce as they were during the

DDT years, and those they saw had probably bred in the Great Lakes. The broad-winged hawk count was the largest we have seen here, consisting of several small "kettles" of the birds whirling above the ridge. Needless to say, the chimney-building played second fiddle to the hawk migration.

SEPTEMBER 19. After another rain during the night, I found a floating green world underfoot and in the air as a dark dawn slowly lit up the earth. Could the drought finally be breaking, washing clean a dry and dusty landscape, scouring it in time for the autumnal equinox?

On the trails today, I discovered that the recent moisture had brought a few mushrooms out of the ground—the usual mushroom-shaped species, unidentifiable except to the experts, and every color of the rainbow. But it also produced several more distinctive kinds that even a novice like me can identify—white coral, giant puffballs, and stinkhorns.

The particular stinkhorn I found (*Phallus ravenelii*) was shaped exactly like the human organ that its genus name suggests, and I could not repress a giggle of amusement. It had a thick white stalk and gray green sticky head with a small opening at the top. They are related to puffballs, earthstars, and bird's nests, all of which produce their spores inside their fruiting bodies. In the case of stinkhorns, the spores are found in the "egg," from which a young stinkhorn develops. When the stinkhorn matures, it elongates and ruptures the "egg," all within a three-hour time span. The "egg" remains at the base of the hollow, stalklike elongation as a volva or tissue that surrounds the developing mushroom, while a slimy layer containing the spores covers the top of the stinkhorn. This gives the mushroom the disagreeable odor for which it is named, but it also attracts insects. They walk all over the sticky spores and distribute them as they move around. As part of my learning experience, I sniffed the stinkhorn and practically choked on the fumes.

Several years ago Steve dated a girl of Lithuanian heritage and learned about the culinary joys of giant puffballs. At his insistence we cooked one by peeling off the skin, slicing it in a circle and then in half, and frying it in margarine. It tasted like some exotic beefsteak rather than like the usual commercial mushroom. So every fall we look for more, and today our son David found two. One weighed well over a pound, the other fourteen ounces— more than enough to satisfy our gourmet palates.

Mushrooms, it turns out, are even more interesting than scientists suspected. They know that the colorful forms we call mushrooms are actually the fruiting bodies of fungi and that each one is sustained by miles of microscopic filaments, called hyphae. Those hyphae snake through the forest floor and into rotting logs, secreting enzymes that break down complex carbohydrates into the nutritive sugars needed by the mushroom. Such saprophytic mushrooms break down woody materials into soil. Without them, our woods would suffocate in their own debris.

The mycologist George Barron and his graduate students at the University of Guelph in Ontario have recently made more remarkable discoveries about what fungi do. Apparently many of them are not benign saprophytes, but fierce predators which attack and eat the microscopic nematodes, rotifers, amoebas, copepods, and bacteria that share the soil with them. And the ways in which they capture and eat them often have the makings of a horror story—catching them in adhesive nets, crushing them with constricting rings, immobilizing them with toxins and eating them alive, attaching to them like tapeworms, impaling them on spores shaped like grappling hooks, and shooting them with projectiles.

Fungi, it turns out, need to have a reasonable balance between the carbon found in carbohydrates and the nitrogen found in protein, about thirty parts of carbon to one part of nitrogen. Wood is generally 500 parts carbon to one part protein, not enough to nourish the fungi. So they must capture microscopic creatures as nitrogen sources.

Barron has only penetrated the tip of what seems to be a very large iceberg, with discoveries of which fungi do what to capture their prey. *Myacena leaiana,* the brilliant orange mushrooms I always find growing in clusters on dead logs at this time of year, feed on bacteria. Other bacteria-eating fungi include the small puffball, turkey tail bracket fungi (which grows on many of our dead logs all year around), and bird's nest mushrooms. But there are many more species that need to be studied.

As usual, the more we learn about the intricate ways of the natural world, the more we realize how much more there is to know. Sadly, with the rapid global destruction of natural habitat, we will never have the chance to learn all that we should.

SEPTEMBER 20. Although it was clear at dawn, with only the rufous-sided towhees and American crows greeting the radiant sunrise, it clouded over rapidly. By the time I started on my walk, it was already totally overcast. But the gloom did not entirely deter the wildlife.

A flock of eight black-capped chickadees called and foraged along Laurel Ridge Trail. A common yellowthroat male scolded from the underbrush, and there were occasional calls from blue jays, red-bellied woodpeckers, white-breasted nuthatches, northern flickers, and Carolina wrens. Mostly, though, the coming silence of winter had settled over the land this brooding day, as if all life had been frozen by the sudden forty-degree cold.

I was stopped by what looked like the remains of a major skirmish along the Far Field Road. A three-foot-wide area had been scraped down to the dirt and was littered with deer prints. A striped maple sapling had had its roots exposed, its trunk scraped of bark, and its leaves and branches ripped off. This signaled that bucks were rubbing the velvet off their antlers, and, in the process, whipping themselves into a frenzy in preparation for the rutting season.

Standing silent and bemused at the spectacle for several minutes, I finally turned toward the Far Field ahead and saw, silhouetted against the edge of the woods, an animal intently watching me. It was a large, gray fox! We looked silently at each other for a few seconds; then it turned and trotted unhurriedly out of sight. All summer we have heard the peculiar barking cry of gray foxes above the Short Circuit Trail, but no matter how many times I had tried to track the sound down, I never found anything. The sole material evidence has been fresh fox scat every day on the trails. But that brief glimpse seemed almost as if it had been a mirage, a figment of my imagination, so badly did I wish to see one. Still, it seemed a good omen for the season ahead, as if at last it *wanted* me to see it.

Steve and Bruce were even luckier. Driving up the hollow from work this evening, they saw a gray fox jump up from its resting place on a gravel pile near the forks where our road divides, one section continuing on up to our place, the other to Margaret's derelict house. They stopped the car to watch as the animal trotted up Margaret's old driveway and settled down on top of a poplar log, its forepaws draped over the front of the log like a dog. There it sat regarding them as quizzically as they regarded it. Finally, Bruce drove on, leaving the fox to its reveries. So when I met them at the door with an account of my gray fox sighting, I was upstaged by theirs. Together we wondered why two of the best sightings we have ever had in over twenty years occurred on the same day and at unlikely times for what is considered to be a crepuscular animal? Furthermore, they were probably two different foxes since the sightings had been so far apart.

SEPTEMBER 21. A beautiful, clear day. The bracken has turned brownish gold on the trails, and leaves filtered down with the slightest breath of air. Gray squirrels shook the largest oak tree limbs or hung upside down from spindly branches—all in pursuit of acorns. They ignored my watching, and if I had been a hunter with a gun in squirrel season, which is coming up soon, most of the squirrels I saw would have been easy to shoot, so intent were they on harvesting, so oblivious to everything around them but the abundance of acorns.

Chipmunks, on the other hand, never gave up their vigilance and "cucked" several hundred times when they spotted me. Bands of blue jays also kept the woods' creatures notified that *someone* was abroad and up to no good.

This afternoon I floated with the clouds and sun and an infinite blue sky atop First Field, but no birds of prey shared my space. Then I walked up into the open thicket on Sapsucker Ridge to be greeted by a bevy of black-capped chickadees and a foraging ruby-crowned kinglet. I also heard many rufous-sided towhees, a pair of northern cardinals, a flock of cedar waxwings, a scolding American robin, house wren chatterings, and lots of odd scratches and rustlings, all hidden by thick underbrush.

An immature red-tailed hawk took off from the base of the powerline right-of-way and sailed low overhead, then higher and higher into the clouds and sunlight until it was lost from view. That hawk and one turkey vulture, both residents, I'm sure, were the only raptors I saw the entire afternoon. Warblers, too, were migrating high in the tree-tops, but only one male black-throated blue warbler came within viewing range.

I dreamt last night that a mountain lion leaped down on me and dug its claws into my back. I never moved, uttering only a silent scream in protest. Then I dreamt that the lumberman's land had been posted against me, and I was told I could never go there again. What kinds of dreams are these? What do they mean?

SEPTEMBER 22. Bruce called them the "silent roto-tillers." Someone else declared it was a buck in rut. I was almost certain it was a mother bear with cubs. But since the last week in August, we have been finding large areas of grass dug up and the sod neatly rolled over. For several weeks I could find no tracks, so I solicited many opinions and did as much reading as I could on what could be destroying our lawns.

Skunks were my first guess, even though my super nose could not detect even a whiff of them. But when huge areas of the lawn were churned up nightly and all the sod I had replaced was torn apart a second, third, and even fourth time, I decided that the amount destroyed in one night was beyond the capacity of skunks.

Finally, last night Bruce fixed our spotlight, and every time I awoke during the night I turned it on and looked out. When I turned it on at 2:00 A.M. I caught them. But they were not skunks or deer or even bears as I had hoped. They lifted their noses from the ground, blinked in the bright light and reared up on their haunches to look around. Their masked faces gave them away. It was a

mother raccoon and her two cubs, or little bears, as raccoons are sometimes called. And they were rooting under
the sod for grubs to eat.

No book I read or person I talked to had ever recorded
such an observation. And I wouldn't have believed it myself if I hadn't caught the culprits with their paws in the
till, so to speak. How little is still known of the lives and
habits of even our most common mammal species.

SEPTEMBER 23. Autumn arrived officially at 8:48 A.M.,
so I went out in the rain to greet it. The hollow dripped
with rain, slowly replenishing the stream. Once again the
road has puddles. One of my favorite poems is Mark Van
Doren's "Morning Worship," and its opening line, "I
wake to hear it raining" has special meaning after the
long, dry summer.

Later several resident black-capped chickadees brought
a flock of visiting warblers through the backyard walnut
trees, or, more likely, the warblers, unfamiliar with local
food sources, were following the chickadees so that they
could hone in quickly on the best feeding areas, stoke up,
and continue on their migration. Recent studies have
shown that migrating songbirds do, indeed, latch on to
resident birds for maximum food in minimum time. Having observed this years ago, I always scan chickadee and
titmice flocks for warblers, vireos, and kinglets at this
time of year.

One warbler flew into our bow window this morning
and lay stunned on the ground. I could see the yellow
rump and brownish back of an immature yellow-rumped
warbler. I ran out to rescue it from the feral cat that was
hunting nearby but had not seen the warbler. As I picked
up the bird, it did not struggle at all. Instead it gaped its
bill open and closed, then blinked its eyes. I took it inside,
all the while smoothing its feathers and talking quietly to

it. Nothing seemed wrong with its wings, and I could not feel the rapid heartbeat of fear that I usually do when I handle an injured bird, probably because it was too new to the world to fear humans. I carried it to the front porch and opened my hand. Away it flew, none the worse for its collision, leaving a bright memory for me. How many people have had the privilege of holding a yellow-rumped warbler in their hand?

SEPTEMBER 24. Mist billowed from the lawn and steamed off the barn roof as the sun warmed the cold ground this morning. Looking down at Sinking Valley, I saw nothing but fog clouds piled up to the level of our mountaintop. It seemed as if there were nothing beyond me, as if I were in an airplane flying blind above the clouds.

I lay back against the Far Field Road bank and looked up into the filtered sunlight to see what I thought at first were hundreds of sunbeams shooting across my line of vision. But they were honeybees, coming and going into the nearby bee tree. I was amazed at their speed, their trajectory, their numbers, but most of all their beauty—flashes of bright light, shooting stars in the daytime sky. So still did I lie, mesmerized by the sight, that an immature red-tailed hawk flew awkwardly in to land on a dead tree close to the bee tree. It paused, looked down at me, and then flew off.

SEPTEMBER 25. Now that the goldenrod is fading, the asters are taking up the slack, humming with honeybees and bumblebees, providing nectar for migrating monarch butterflies. Aster, both its common and genus name, is Greek for "star," and so "starwort" is the older name for the flowers. They are "stars fetched from the night skies and planted on the fields of day," according to William A.

Quayle's description written back in the first decade of the twentieth century.[5]

Most of our asters are faded blue in color and grow in masses among the goldenrod, especially at the Far Field. Such asters are as difficult to identify as the many species of goldenrod. Harold William Rickett in his definitive *Wildflowers of the United States, the Northeastern States* separated out forty-nine species of asters in our area.

Like goldenrod, many species of asters have interbred, further confusing the issue, but there is no mistaking the beautiful purple-stemmed aster (*Aster puniceus*) which grows down at the base of First Field in our small wetland. Other purple-flowered asters which are easy to identify are the large-leaved aster (*Aster macrophyllus*), with its heart-shaped leaves, and wavy-leaved aster (*Aster undulatus*). The latter has distinctive winged leaf stalks which expand into lobes that clasp the stem. Both species grow in the woods along our road bank, their pale purple blossoms a contrast to the predominant woods' species, the white wood aster (*Aster divaricatus*). It too has heart-shaped leaves but they are on stalks.

Because so many white asters of various species are the last of the blooming wildflowers, often hanging on until November, the whole group is often referred to as "frostweeds." These stout, bushy plants with myriad tiny, white, daisylike blossoms, have yellow centers that usually turn reddish-brown after they are fertilized, but still they go on blooming, "for they come as the frost comes, as a breath upon the landscape, a silver rime of chill flowering in the old age of the year," as Donald Culross Peattie wrote in *An Almanac for Moderns* (p. 183).

So I sat this glorious day among the asters at the edge of the Far Field, listening to calling crows and basking in

---

5. As cited by Durant, *Who Named the Daisy?*, p. 10.

the sunlight. It seemed, at the time, the most wonderful activity I could engage in. No wonder wild animals and domestic ones too, spend so much of their time similarly engaged while we humans continue to lay up treasures for ourselves on earth, taking heed of the morrow instead of appreciating the moment at hand.

SEPTEMBER 26. Immature raptors sure get themselves into trouble during the autumn when they are still learning the ropes. Most don't even live through their first year, since learning to be a really effective predator is difficult. This morning I heard a commotion in the yard and stepped outside to find a flock of blue jays in the black walnut trees harassing an immature sharp-skinned hawk. The little accipiter flew around the yard, closely followed by half a dozen blue jays, a couple of which dove at it. Then it landed on the driveway and screamed back at the jays several times before finally flying off over the shed lawn and disappearing.

The wind picked up by afternoon, and Steve went up to look for raptors from what we call the "amphitheater," a semicircular depression above the house and halfway up First Field below Sapsucker Ridge. Before I joined him he had a wonderful view of the first ever peregrine falcon for the mountain. He even saw its mask as it came low over the ridgetop. Otherwise, his count for less than two hours, between 2:00 and 4:00 P.M., was three sharp-skinned hawks, four red-tailed hawks, one northern harrier, and four turkey vultures. Steve did all the work of finding the birds and adjusting the spotting scope, rousing me from my recumbent position each time. How absolutely beautiful it was lying in the field still glowing with goldenrod, watching the scudding clouds and the monarch butterflies spiraling high up against the sky like small birds.

As I relaxed there, I was reminded of a religious radio program I had listened to the other night. Listening to such programs is not my usual inclination, but the host had been praised to me as someone who cared about families and about nature, so I tuned in. His guests were Canadian naturalists, people I had never heard of. Children, they maintained, see wonder in the natural world, a wonder *all* of us lose when we lose our childlike innocence. (So what does that make me—Peter Pan?) Then they denied the existence of evolution, claiming that as Christians they could not believe in the creation of the earth as science explains it. I was surprised at their attitude. Can't the heavens be telling the glory of God through the miraculous intricateness of evolution? The more we learn about how the natural world works, the more we should be filled with wonder and praise. The knowledge that our green earth is a mere pinprick in the vastness of the universe and we a mere blink of the eye in geological time should make us humble.

SEPTEMBER 27. Breezy, beautiful, but with an autumnal chill in the air, so I sought the sunshine rather than the shade for walking and sitting. Rufous-sided towhees foraged in the underbrush, a ruffed grouse exploded from the laurel cover, but, best of all, I spotted the first winter wren of the season, bouncing along the stream bank in the hollow. Late September and October are the months when winter wrens migrate south from the conifer forests of the north where they prefer to mate and raise their families.

Today the tiny winter wren, sporting a dark brown back, heavily barred belly, and stub of a tail, stood on a fallen branch and bobbed up and down like an animated toy. I remained still as it continued alternately bobbing and poking about the leaf litter in search of the insects it relished. It also kept an eye on me but did not seem upset by my presence. This is a characteristic of winter wrens. While they are often difficult to find because of their preference for low tangles, once one is spotted it tends to be both inquisitive and fearless. One researcher even reported that a winter wren had landed right on him—he was wearing a brown suit at the time.

The winter wren (*Troglodytes troglodytes*) is the same species the English call just plain "wren." But the common American name is apt since the bird sometimes spends its winters in the north. Its scientific name means "cave dweller," referring to its cavelike nest, hollowed into the earth of uprooted trees, under the bark of trees, or beneath stream banks.

We first noticed the winter wren's propensity for uprooted trees and stream banks after the small tornado cut a swath through the woods above the stream ten years ago. By late summer of that same year, winter wrens could be seen flitting through the underbrush beneath the fallen trees.

All through the autumn and winter months we caught glimpses of them, and during the Christmas Bird Count we saw another one in a grape tangle two miles from the tornado site. Since then, there is usually at least one wintering down along the stream bank. So, some winter wrens do stay in central Pennsylvania during the cold months. But we have yet to find any nesting. I have my hopes, though, because one observer back in 1893 reported that "in the Alleghenies where our most magnificent shrubs, rhododendrons, mountain laurel or kalmias, and different azaleas fringe the streams and brooks and often cover whole mountainsides, lending to them an indescribable charm, this bird appears to take up its abode everywhere"—an apt description of our hollow environment.[6]

6. Henry Nehrling as cited by Arthur Cleveland Bent, Life Histories of North American Nuthatches, Wrens, Thrashers, and Their Allies, p. 148.

Cordelia Stanwood, a bird photographer and observer of nests, who lived in Ellsworth, Maine, did much pioneering work in the study of nesting winter wrens. She called them "spirits of the brooks," referring to their song, which she described as a "high, cold blast. It suggests the rippling, trickling of the little brooks made by the melting ice and snow," she wrote in her journal on April 15, 1911.

Winter wrens that do go south to warmer climes are among the earliest birds to reappear, because they migrate no farther than Florida. By April 5 they have reached Harrisburg, Pennsylvania, and, as Stanwood reported, they reappear along coastal Maine by mid-April. She watched two winter wren nests and observed that the female alone builds the nest, incubates the eggs, and feeds the nestlings. The male stays close by, singing and occasionally feeding the female, and he helps to feed the young after they have fledged. He also keeps himself busy by sometimes building as many as four dummy nests.

The female feeds the nestlings as often as once a minute, from dawn until dusk, giving them moths, crane flies, cutworms, caterpillars, and spiders. Usually they leave the nest in nineteen days, but they continue traveling about as a family for several weeks.

When the family group breaks up, winter wrens resume what seems to be a most solitary life. They leave Maine as late as November 5 and have been seen migrating through our area as late as November 23. This bouncy, brown mite with its penetrating call, is a welcome companion during the autumn and winter months, so I was glad to see the first of what should be several dozen over the next several weeks.

SEPTEMBER 28. A golden autumn day, breezy, blue-skied, and cloudless. Overnight the black walnut leaves have turned yellow, and viewed against the blue sky they are a molten marvel.

I discovered, at the top of First Field, a pair of praying mantises preparing to mate on a Norway spruce sapling. Or perhaps they were already finished. In any case, although the smaller, brown male had his front legs clasped around the larger green female, they were not connected in any way as I discovered when I nudged them.

This particular species of mantis, the native *Stagmomantis carolina*, is as predatory as the approximately eighteen hundred other, mostly tropical, species throughout the world, the only Orthopteran (which includes grasshoppers, crickets, roaches, and walking sticks) that prefers animal rather than plant protein. Praying mantis females are notorious for their cannibalistic habit of eating their mates after mating, so I wondered if, by interfering, I had interrupted their nuptials just in time?

Scientists have discovered that after one or several matings, the female attaches herself to an appropriate stem and begins her combination nest-making and egg-laying, a process that takes at least three hours, according to the late naturalist, Edwin Way Teale. As Teale described it in *Grassroot Jungles:* "Like toothpaste coming from a tube, the whitish, gummy material of which the egg case is composed squeezes from the tip of the insect's abdomen. Tiny appendages, whirling at high speed, beat it into froth. . . . As the work advances, the tip of the abdomen moves back and forth in a slow, expanding oval, building up the egg case much as a threshing machine builds up a strawstack. At regular intervals, the eggs are laid in this mass of froth" (p. 50).

Teale, it turns out, kept numerous praying mantises as pets in his study. The most famous and long-lived he called Dinah. She had as much curiosity and personality as a pet cat, and, like a pet cat, could be fierce in defending her rights, even against creatures much larger than herself. She also had an amazing appetite. For a while, in late summer and early autumn, Teale was able to catch enough live insects, supplemented with hamburger, to keep Dinah satiated. But as the weather grew colder, he grew more desperate and resorted to feeding her insects that had been paralyzed in a jar of ammonia fumes. She seemed to relish them, smacking her palps when she finished. Next, he gave her two wasps from his cyanide killing bottle, reeking with poisonous fumes. She loved them.

Emboldened by his experiment in praying mantises' tastes and tolerance for poisons, he next offered her an insect that had been packed in dichlorbenzol, the chemical used to make moth balls. She waited for the odor to dissipate in the open air for a few minutes and then gobbled it down. Finally, the next day, he offered her the culminating *pièce de résistance,* a wasp that had been killed in the cyanide jar, dipped in shellac, and then soaked in 195-proof denatured alcohol. "She downed it with relish and wiped her mouth and washed her face and looked around for more," Teale reported.[7] Dinah eventually expired, not because of her tastes but because of old age. Praying mantises are programmed to die in autumn after procreation and egg-laying. Those several hundred eggs are perfectly protected in their hardened cases so that the next generation, which hatches in early spring, can begin the cycle all over again.

Whenever I see a praying mantis turn its head around and seemingly peer intently at me, I am reminded of Dinah and am tempted to find my own pet. But as Teale admitted, he had had many before Dinah, and none had been as fearless and companionable. Praying mantises, it

7. Teale, *Near Horizons,* pp. 290–91.

seems, can be as individualistic as many, higher forms of wild creatures.

SEPTEMBER 29. On this dark gloomy day I was rewarded with a feast of wild turkey watching. As I neared the Far Field I spotted a large flock of turkeys ahead of me on the road. I counted seven, but I could not see the whole range of the flock before they sensed my presence and moved off, flexing their wings. They did not fly, though, but merely walked away, so I thought that they had not seen my frozen form and had been reacting, instead, to a cawing crow.

When I reached the Far Field, it was a maze of turkey heads craning above the high weeds. This time I counted sixteen, and I'm sure I missed quite a few. Slowly they ambled through the field, nibbling on goldenrod where, I suspect, they were finding insect food. I skulked slowly and quietly forward, and most of them moved off except for seven that stayed nearby in the black locust grove at the edge of the field, foraging and craning their necks until they too finally melted off into the woods, drawn by the soft clucking, presumably, of their mother. At this time of year several hen turkeys often team up with their young, so what I saw was probably the current offspring of about three families.

By evening the sky had cleared. We watched the full moon through a large telescope a friend had lent us, in search of the occasional zip of a migrating songbird flying across the moon's path.

SEPTEMBER 30. I am struck by the silence and darkness of autumn mornings. No longer am I awakened by birdsongs and bright sunshine. Instead, it is dark and great horned owls are hooting.

Later, with the coming of light, the eastern phoebes call for several minutes. Then the rufous-sided towhees, hidden in the grape tangle, chime in with their "chewinks." Once the sun has risen, the American goldfinches gather in droves to eat the thistles that have gone to seed along the driveway.

It has been a great year both for thistles and goldfinches, and this morning I stood watching them as they bounced between thistle plants and the dying Seckel pear tree. Then I looked closer and spotted several magnolia warblers also feeding in the pear tree. Like yellow-rumped warblers, magnolia warblers have a yellow rump mark, but they also have yellow breasts and a band of white in the middle of their black tails.

I continued up our road to look for the mourning dove I discovered there several days ago bobbing along. At first I had thought it was unusually bold. But once I caught up with it, it attempted to fly and couldn't. Still, it was nimble enough to stay out of reach, so I let it go its way each time I saw it. I had never before been close enough to a mourning dove to see its thin blue eye ring and to admire the unexpected subtlety of browns and grays on its wings and back. Today it is gone so I have no idea whether its wing was healed or a predator finally caught it.

In the afternoon, I heard the first of the Canada geese flying overhead. The second flock, a large, wavering V of at least one hundred, went over at six o'clock in the evening. That flock was closely followed by another and, after dark, I heard still another flock through the walls of the house. To hear geese in the spring is wonderful; to hear them in the fall is poignant because they presage the ending of warmth and verdure.

October

It comes quietly as mist in the night, but it doesn't vanish as the sun rises. It remains, stronger day after day. It spreads, leaf to leaf, branch to branch, tree to tree. It climbs from the valley to the hilltop. Soon it will possess the countryside. . . . We sum it all up in two words: The Color.

—Hal Borland,
Twelve Moons of the Year

OCTOBER 1. I had to be away for the entire day with Bruce and Steve, something I really did not want to do when I'm keeping a full chronicle of the autumn. Then, coming home near dark, Bruce found that our new lock had been smashed and left lying on our gate latch.

We had originally put up the gate at the bottom of the hollow to keep out "midnight dumpers" who had several times deposited household trash, including an old television set, in our stream. In the first year, the gate had been vandalized a number of times until, one day, it was stolen altogether. Some friends had helped us put in a sturdy, steel, vandal-proof gate, but we could not find a vandal-proof lock. The previous lock had been smashed in July, and oddly enough that one was also left on top of the gate latch, like an offering to appease us.

As we drove up the hollow, Bruce recalled that when our friend had talked with the lumberman about buying the property earlier in the summer, the lumberman had mentioned prospective buyers who had looked at the land in July. Since that was about when we found the previously smashed lock, Steve immediately concluded that the lumberman was responsible for both broken locks. But I refused to believe it. Despite our difference of opinion concerning logging, he seemed to be an honorable, law-abiding man. Surely he would not stoop to vandalism. Steve admitted he didn't know him as well as I did, but he stuck to his opinion. Bruce was ambivalent and did not know what to believe.

OCTOBER 2. We pondered the question overnight, discouraged that once again we would have to buy a new lock and supply keys to emergency crews, friends, and utility companies, as we had done so many times over the past five years.

This beautiful autumn morning I sat outside on the veranda drinking coffee and heard what sounded like a bulldozer over on our lumberman-neighbor's land, so I walked down to the fork in our road to see if I could figure out what was happening. I could see nothing as I looked up at Margaret's derelict house, but it sounded as if the bulldozer was going back down the ridge along the access road the lumberman had built.

When I got back to the house, the telephone was ringing. It was Bruce calling from town. He and Steve had encountered the lumberman's son driving up the road, and he admitted he had smashed the lock yesterday so that he could get a logging crew up the road. Steve had been right after all.

Bruce asked me to call the state police and have them send a trooper to meet us at the gate to file a report. Then

I drove down the hollow with the smashed lock. The lumberman's son stuck around and admitted to the trooper he had done it—with only three hammer blows, he said, adding that it was amazing how cheaply locks were made today. The whole scene was weird. Bruce said that he was going to put another lock on the gate, but he urged the son to tell his father that he really wanted to resolve the issues between us. Why didn't his father return calls? Why didn't he respond to letters? The man looked uncomfortable.

"Did your father tell you to smash the lock?" Bruce asked.

"He told me to get through the gate in any way I could," he responded. He also claimed that his father had ordered him and the rest of the crew to stay 200 feet above the road, using the Lower Road as a rough boundary line. Furthermore, he admitted that they had access to their work site along their haul road through the neighbor's property, but using the hollow road was faster and easier.

Bruce asked the trooper if we could press charges—perhaps that would prompt the lumberman to respond to our concerns—and the trooper agreed. Then, to our surprise, the son suddenly stuck out his hand to Bruce and said he hoped there weren't any hard feelings! Bruce obligingly shook his hand, but he repeated to him that he hoped his father would deal with the issues and answer his letters. And so we left it.

But my peace of mind was blown away. After six years of changing their story, what was really going to happen? Once they had offered to sell the land to us; then they wouldn't. Next they said they were only going to remove the trees killed by gypsy moths. That statement was amended to include all trees over twelve inches in diameter. Now will they even stick to the careful, selective cut they had promised so often, I wondered. Will they respect the 200-foot boundary they agreed upon almost two years ago? Will the lumberman ever confirm that agreement with us?

But in my heart I already suspect what will happen. After so many false starts and threats, this time they mean to totally clear out their property. The beautiful hollow will be destroyed and perhaps the road as well. All those wonderful areas I found last winter, particularly the large trees on the wilderness knoll, will be gone in a few weeks. Autumn, it seems, is the season of rapine around here, which makes it difficult to appreciate the beauty.

Suddenly, autumn has become a time of intense sorrow for me. The brilliant leaf colors seem to symbolize the final flare before the inevitable end—a bright flame, consuming itself like a candle, leaving nothing but a burnt-out, trashed, and dying earth.

To escape the scream of chain saws and skidders, I walked this afternoon to my usual refuge—the Far Field Road. Gray squirrels fed as I sat and watched, soothing my spirits as they went about their business, unperturbed by my presence. Walking back on the Far Field Trail, I saw an ovenbird fly across in front of me and land on a log where it skulked along on its long, elegant, pink legs in usual ovenbird fashion.

Then, as I descended First Field through the locust grove, I heard a high-pitched "cree-cree-cree-cree." An osprey circled above me, a fish clasped in its talons, both fish and osprey facing in the same direction. The raptor made several passes over the field before it flew to a tree branch on Sapsucker Ridge where it stood and looked around silently while I sat down in the locust grove and watched it through my binoculars. Its white head and black eye stripe gleamed in the sunlight, and it looked almost as if a black hood extended down the back of its neck. Whenever a pileated woodpecker called, the osprey glanced around alertly, but otherwise it sat there quietly, looking off into the distance and completely ignoring the fish in its talons.

I felt a hushed charm as I kept it company, but after half an hour I finally broke the spell by trying to see how close I could get to the osprey before it flew. As I walked nearer, it began calling again. Leaning forward, it gave me an excellent view of its snowy underparts. At last it flew directly overhead, still holding the brown fish, probably a trout from the river at the base of our mountain. Then it was off over Laurel Ridge, gone from view in a few seconds, having given me my closest and longest encounter ever with an osprey.

OCTOBER 3. The first "snowbirds" returned today, fluttering down on our driveway and flashing their white and gray tail feathers. Otherwise known as dark-eyed juncos (*Junco hyemalis*), they spend the spring and summer farther north in the cool forests of Canada and Alaska or in the high Appalachians as far south as northern Georgia. Although they prefer to court and raise their families in hemlock-studded ravines in northern and western Pennsylvania, I have never found any in our hemlock-lined hollow during the spring and summer months. For that reason, I think of them as winter birds along with American tree sparrows, pine siskins, and evening grosbeaks.

Their color pattern is often described as "leaden skies above, snow below," referring to their dark gray heads and backs and white bellies, a striking combination that dulls into touches of brown in both the juveniles and females. But all dark-eyed juncos possess distinctive white outer tail feathers. Juncos are feeder birds, although they usually scratch on the ground beneath instead of landing on my hanging feeder. Since they prefer brushy edge habitats for winter feeding, they spend much of their time in the grape tangle below our back porch, less than six feet away from the seed that spills from the feeder.

Those first arrivals probably wintered here last year, and their presence will attract more migrants. By early December a whole flock of dark-eyed juncos, with a fixed foraging range, will be assembled on our grounds for the winter. So I can be almost certain that the birds at my feeder are the same ones from day to day.

The flock will not always travel together, but it will respect the boundary lines of other foraging flocks. Researchers have found that all members of a single flock do recognize each other and have a definite, quite simple pecking order. The kingpin is A, who is dominant over B and all others, while B is dominant over C and all others, and so on down the alphabet. Dominant birds peck at or chase the subordinates. They may also stretch out their bodies, close their bills, and bob their heads up and down, actions that anyone watching a bird feeder can observe.

The subordinate birds are those that always fly off quickly when other juncos, presumably the dominant ones, come in for food. Sometimes they do fight, either by running at a rival on the ground or by flying up into the air, face to face. Apparently, sex does not determine the pecking order; females have often been observed driving males from feeders.

Back in 1957, Winifred S. Sabine of Ithaca, New York, reported in *The Auk,* journal of the American Ornithologists' Union, that after their last feeding foray of the day, dark-eyed juncos always left in a regular pattern. Each bird would finish eating, pause for a moment or two, then join the rest of the flock in an arbor vitae bush forty feet away. When all were assembled they flew off together in the same direction toward their common night roost— in dense evergreens, thickets, or brush piles.

For years our feeder juncos preferred a thick barberry

hedge between the shed and guesthouse which twittered with disturbed birds whenever we passed at dusk. There were many old bird nests to sleep in and impenetrable thorns to keep predators out, so they had a safe spot to drowse away the long, cold nights. Then, the small juniper bush we planted in the herb garden, less than ten feet away from the feeder, shot up to ten feet and became the juncos' new night roost. They never fly in there just once every evening, however. Instead, they go in and out, adjusting and readjusting their positions until the bush is fairly bursting with juncos. Watching them from the hall window a foot away provides great entertainment.

The juncos that do not come to our feeder but do spend the winter on the mountain, and there can be several hundred of them, head for the Norway spruce grove at the top of First Field. One winter day near dusk I sat quietly in the midst of several large trees. Juncos zipped in one by one, more and more as the light faded. Many circled above my head. Others retreated just before slamming into me and then sat on nearby branches to scold. Judging from the feces dotting the limbs around me, I was sitting close to a favorite roosting spot. Finally, I stood up and walked away so they could settle onto their rightful branches before dark. Juncos, like many people, are creatures of habit, and to disturb them is to endanger their survival. Once the colors of autumn have faded and all the migrant birds have gone, dark-eyed juncos come into their own. To hear their twitters and trills, to watch them scratch beneath the feeder, to see them on a snowy morning is to appreciate their indomitable spirits.

OCTOBER 4. The skidder was screaming away shortly after 8:00 A.M., the chain saws providing a growling undertone, while the crash of enormous trees reverberated from ridgetop to ridgetop, as if the falling trees were a few yards away. Weary and depressed, I fled to the Far Field to sit with my back against a huge wild black cherry tree and enjoy the peace.

I heard behind me a running animal and assumed it was another gray squirrel, but I remained motionless, hoping it would come near. The animal passed within a foot of me, still running hard, reached the edge of the field, veered left, ran as far as the beginning of a locust grove, turned around for a few seconds in my direction, and then trotted off into the tall weeds of the Far Field. It was, to my utter shock and startlement, a gray fox! I could have reached out and grabbed it had I thought it was anything other than chasing squirrels. Once again this peaceful haven, far from the sounds of lumbering, offered me sudden joy as an antidote for my gloomy thoughts.

The autumn color is glorious this year. Deep gold spice bushes are covered with shiny red berries. The blueberry shrubs on the powerline right-of-way have turned a deep reddish purple. The black gum trees glow in shades of pink, rose, red, and reddish purple, creating an understory haze of color along Laurel Ridge.

Although poets praise the autumnal beauty of New England's sugar maples, no one, so far as I can determine, has similarly immortalized the color of Pennsylvania's black gum trees. Yet despite their plain oval leaves, black gums decked out in Burgundy red are as brilliant as sugar maples. However, they reach their peak nearly a month before most trees color.

Scientists, who are always asking why, have known for years that certain trees, shrubs, and vines take on vibrant hues a full month before the majority of the woody plants withdraw the green chlorophyll from their leaves. And they can easily explain how color change occurs in all deciduous growth.

But they have been unable to agree on why some plants change color weeks before others, flooding their leaves with the enzyme that breaks down chlorophyll and transports certain chemicals, such as nitrogen and magnesium, out of the leaves before they drop. This process unveils the red, orange, yellow, and brown pigments that have been in the leaves all along and gives our Appalachian forests their worldwide reputation for flaming color.

Black gum, also known as sour gum, black tupelo, and pepperidge, favors swampy woods, hence its lyrical scientific name—*Nyssa sylvatica,* meaning "water nymph of the forest." But according to William Carey Grimm's *The Trees of Pennsylvania,* black gum trees are also common on dry mountain ridges, burned-over forests, and abandoned fields. Because their heartwood rots early, they are primarily understory trees with an average height of thirty to forty feet.

Here on our dry Appalachian mountaintop, occasional black gum leaves turn red in late August, and by early September the understory is aflame with them. Hidden beneath their flamboyantly colored leaves, are small clusters of half-inch long, bluish black fruits. Two other understory species that color early are flowering dogwood and sassafras. Flowering dogwood has leaves that are primarily purplish red and showy clusters of red fruit, while sassafras has yellow and red leaves and dark blue, shiny fruits, each of which grows on a club-shaped, bright red stalk.

At the same time, Virginia creeper, sporting flat-topped clusters of bluish black fruits, entwines both dead and living trees with ropes of scarlet, and wild grapevines, bearing compact clumps of purplish berries, smother our thickets in molten gold. The spicebushes lining our stream are covered with bright yellow leaves and clusters of red fruits, and the poison ivy that grows in our old corral has leaves ranging in color from yellow and orange to red and produces creamy white, small, berrylike clusters of fruit. The occasional staghorn sumac shrubs at the edge of First Field also turn color early, displaying a deep red to match their five- to eight-inch-long, erect, conical fruit clusters.

Several years ago, Edmund W. Stiles, a biologist at Rutgers University, offered a plausible explanation of early leaf coloring. He had been studying wild fruits and their relationship to birds as consumers and seed dispersers and had discovered that in the summer, when birds lay eggs, grow new feathers, and raise their families, they seem to prefer eating high protein insects. During those times, small fruits such as blueberries, blackberries, and cherries that are high in sugars and other carbohydrates are a second food choice.

But with the onset of migration in late summer, birds begin looking for foods that are high in lipids, or fats, presumably to fuel their long flights. At the same time, many of the plants bearing fat-rich fruits turn color. Furthermore, seasonal bird migrators do include such major fruit-eating species as American robins, cedar waxwings, eastern bluebirds, veeries, brown thrashers, gray catbirds, and hermit, Swainson's, gray-cheeked, and wood thrushes.

Stiles points out that migrating birds are moving through new territory and are not familiar with food sources available along the way. So he hypothesizes that the contrast of colored leaves against a mostly still green forest signals the presence of food to the birds. Hence he has coined a new term for plants that turn color early and coincidentally also have ripe fruit. He calls them "foliar fruit flags." Not surprisingly, the prominent members of this group in the Pennsylvania Appalachians are black gum, flowering dogwood, sassafras, spicebush, Virginia creeper, poison ivy, sumac, and wild grape.

Are those plants signaling to fruit-eating bird migrators the presence of food? Because they have fruits with seeds that need to be dispersed by birds, it seems a likely explanation.

Moreover, the fruit of spicebush, flowering dogwood, black gum, and sassafras are uniformly high in lipids, so the birds are doing themselves a favor by rapidly consuming them. The birds also perform a service for those plants, because fruits high in lipids rot quickly. For that reason they need to be eaten relatively soon and then passed through the birds' digestive systems while the seeds are still viable.

Many foliar fruit flag plants have another characteristic in common. With the exception of sumac and flowering dogwood, their berries are inconspicuous and hidden by leaves. So without their colored leaves, the birds might not see the fruit. In addition, the fruiting vines, Stiles maintains, are especially difficult to spot when they are green and twining along trunks and tree branches or vining on the ground in the weeds and grasses. But when the vines turn color, they are strikingly beautiful and easy to see.

So, if Stiles is right, bird migration, plant dispersal and early leaf color are linked together, demonstrating once again that in nature everything is connected to everything else, in intricate and often little-understood ways, producing a finely tuned system that has continued to evolve over the millennia. To destroy even one link may be disastrous to an entire system. Probably it is only incidental that such processes as leaf color, early or late, also present a feast for humans' eyes and a boost to their spirits.

OCTOBER 5. A flock of American robins came into the yard this morning, and the eastern bluebirds were back and calling, having raised their two families in our bluebird box and then disappeared for a month or so. Since they do this every year, I never worry about them, knowing that they will return, often with friends, to grace the latter days of autumn with their color.

It was warm enough to have our Saturday breakfast on the front porch, and little birds called from the treetops still hidden by leaves. But later, the slightest breeze set the black walnut leaves whirling through the air like a shower of golden confetti. Already the black walnuts in the front yard are naked while the backyard trees are still half-clothed but shedding fast—the last to leaf out in the spring, the first to lose their leaves in the fall, they are more often leafless than leaved in a year.

Since the lumberman and his forester had repeatedly invited us to inspect their work, Bruce and I decided to walk over and take a look. They have bulldozed their way far along the ridgetop and have cut magnificent, huge, 150-year-old red oak trees all the way. Two new roads have been built straight down the steep mountainside, one connected to the Upper Road, the other aiming for the end of the Upper Road where the wonderful knoll of huge trees is—my wilderness grove discovery of last winter. The roads were deep in dry soil, and my boots were as dusty as if I had been walking in the Peruvian desert. The ridge was hot and open now to the burning sun. Much of the ridge road was rocky, the earth quickly scraped away from the soil-thin mountaintop. So many years to build a little soil up there; a few minutes with a bulldozer to destroy it.

Mosquitoes, more than I had seen all summer, rose in clouds from the freshly churned-up dirt. Altogether, what has been done so far is a lesson in devastation. Our one hope is that they may cut only the largest trees and let the rest alone. But the destruction to the soil and to the smaller shrubs, trees, and creatures underneath the bulldozer and skidder is incredibly wasteful. If we have torrential rains, a good portion of what little soil there is will wash away down the mountainside.

So much scarring of the natural world for profit, so little beauty left to nourish the spirit, not only here but throughout the world. Is that why people have less and less spirituality and more and more worship of materialism in their lives no matter what their formal ties to religion are?

By afternoon, back on our own property, the day glowed, activating birds into song and causing butterflies to beat against the windows—the kind of gleaming day more often dreamed of than experienced. I put our morning horror show behind me and faced into the warm wind, streaming with falling leaves. A male American kestrel sat on the telephone wire directly above the bluebird box. He looked small and polite and shy as he peered around—a quiet, seemingly unpredatory creature as serene as the afternoon. The fields sizzled and popped with grasshoppers, crickets, and katydids. Patches of late goldenrod still gleamed and attracted the dozens and dozens of migrating monarchs fluttering over the mountaintop.

I stood on top of Laurel Ridge and watched them as they came out of the northeast, up and over the powerline right-of-way and down into our goldenrod-covered First Field to make a short nectaring stop before heading purposefully south. Because monarch butterflies originated in a warmer climate, they cannot tolerate any long periods of cold weather. Instead of adapting to the cold, they flee from it like so many of our birds do.

A monarch butterfly begins its life as a minute, pearly egg laid by a female on a freshly emerging leaf or flower bud of one of the 108 species of milkweed growing in North America. Milkweed is its larval food as a caterpillar, and each larva requires a large number of leaves to complete its development. To reduce the competition, as soon as a caterpillar hatches, it immediately eats any other eggs it finds on its milkweed. Then it feeds on the milkweed until it pupates. In a short time it makes its final transition into an adult. This whole process from egg to adult takes between three and five weeks, depending on the temperature, and produces up to three and possibly four generations of monarch butterflies by the end of summer.

But, by then, a change has occurred. The last generation of monarchs in mid-August is so influenced by the decreased day length and colder night temperatures that their neuroendocrine systems produce a juvenile hormone. This hormone represses the mating urge in the male and egg production in the female, a state known as reproductive diapause, a period of reproductive dormancy. Not only do the adult ovaries and testes of the butterflies remain immature, but the butterflies are not interested in sex or milkweeds, and the process of aging is greatly slowed down. Instead of using their energies to produce another generation, they begin to feed heavily on the nectar of fall composite flowers. In addition, they join in social nectaring assemblages during the day and form temporary clusters at night. One August I observed a few small clusters hanging from our black walnut trees, but during migration, which usually begins in mid-September, I see only solitary butterflies.

Like migrating birds, monarchs also need lipids (fats) to give them energy not only before but during their migration. They obtain them through drinking flower nectar which they convert and store in a specialized fat body, an abdominal organ similar to our liver. As they near their wintering ground, they store even more lipids, since wildflowers at those wintering sites deteriorate and can't provide enough nectar for the butterflies.

Since 1930 scientists had known that monarchs migrate and, in fact, large clusters of western North American monarchs spend their winters clinging to favorite trees in about forty California sites along the coastline from north of San Francisco to south of Los Angeles, the most famous being in Pacific Grove. A few smaller assemblages had also been discovered in Florida, presumably a portion of the monarchs from the northeastern United States and Canada. Where, though, did the majority of the eastern monarch butterflies winter?

Fred A. Urquhart of Scarborough College in Toronto was determined to find out. In 1952 he formed the Insect Migration Association, and interested people tagged monarchs by the thousands. From those that were later recovered, they learned that almost all male monarchs die on their way back north in the spring and that monarchs do not fly at night. But their most interesting discovery was that most eastern monarchs migrate from the Northeast to the Southwest, converging on Texas. However, the butterflies could be seen flying farther south, convincing Urquhart that their destination was somewhere in central Mexico.

In 1973 he advertised in a Mexico City newspaper, asking for help in locating the overwintering home of the eastern monarch butterflies. Ken Brugger, an American living in Mexico, responded. In his van, accompanied by his new Mexican bride, he crisscrossed central Mexico for two winters, talking to herders who kept cattle in the Sierra Madre. At last, on January 9, 1975, responding to a local rumor, he discovered *millions* of monarch butterflies on a twenty-acre site in the mountains. They were clinging to Oyamel fir trees that grow at an elevation of 9,000 feet. As one naturalist later wrote, "The clusters . . . sculptured the Mexican highlands into pulsating cathedrals of tiny stained glass windows."[1]

Fred Urquhart was elated. With the help of Brugger, he had finally found the major wintering grounds of the

1. George, "My Search for Secret Agent #25238," p. 16.

eastern monarch butterflies. For some of those butterflies it is a twenty-four-hundred-mile migration, and when they reach central Mexico, they cling to trees in a semi-dormant state for most of the winter. This conserves their body heat, since temperatures in the area range from below to just above freezing. To see them then is a wondrous sight. Lincoln Brower, a scientist who has been studying monarch butterflies for many years, described it as "a wall of butterflies. Great draperies hung over the branches, turning them into giant feather dusters, and the trunks were softly wrapped with tightly packed rows of thousands of monarchs clinging to each other and to the bark."[2]

In February, when the temperature begins to rise, the mating and egg production hormones kick in again, and at least some of the butterflies mate at their wintering grounds. They leave the overwintering sites from the middle to the end of March, flying rapidly northeast into the southern United States and continuing courtship and mating along the migration routes and after they arrive in the southern states. According to Brower, the spring recolonization of eastern North America by monarch butterflies is a two-step process. First the overwintering butterflies breed in the south and produce a new generation. It is that generation which continues the migration north when it becomes too hot, in mid-June, for another generation to develop successfully there.

This leads to another monarch mystery that has still to be solved. The monarchs that migrate in autumn are not the same ones that returned from the south. How do they find their way? All scientists can say is that the urge to migrate has to be inherited and that the migration itself involves orientational and navigational responses to un-

2. Brower, "A Royal Voyage to an Enchanted Forest," p. 28.

known cues which can lead the butterflies all the way from Maine to approximately twelve small relict Oyamel fir forests in the remote mountains of central Mexico, seventy-five miles west of Mexico City.

Life is not easy on their wintering grounds, however. Two species of birds, the black-headed grosbeak and the black-backed oriole, eat thousands a day during clear and warm weather. But the weather is not always warm and clear. When it drops below freezing, many monarchs die. Fifty percent perish when their body temperature is lowered to 18 degrees Fahrenheit and 100 percent at 5 degrees. Sometimes storms last for days, and at such times the ground is littered with dead and dying butterflies.

But at is true everywhere today, the greatest threats to monarch butterfly survival, both in Mexico and California, are caused by humanity. In Mexico people press further and further into the mountains in search of land to graze their cattle and wood to cut for fuel and profits; in California it is real estate development that threatens the remaining sites, several of which have already been destroyed. Lately, Mexico has moved strongly to protect its sites, led by Mexican conservationists. Similar efforts have been launched in California.

I hope they will succeed. If I never get to Mexico to see them in their overwintering sites, I can at least look forward to a continual feast of monarch butterfly beauty during their summer and early autumn time here on our mountain.

OCTOBER 6. A storm and wind cleared the skies and lowered the temperature overnight, and it was forty-three degrees this morning. Warblers—black-throated greens, Nashvilles, and those I could not see well enough to identify, moved through the yard early today. The Far Field thicket was filled with migrating birds—white-throated sparrows, rufous-sided towhees, solitary vireos, ruby-crowned kinglets, and more black-throated green warblers. Both the kinglets and the vireos came to feed on the wild grapevines close to where I was sitting. One ruby-crowned kinglet even dipped his head and showed off his red crown as he foraged. Those species are bolder than others, not minding my nearness and audible expressions of wonder.

Bird migration is still mysterious even though researchers have been making progress in unraveling its complexities by using a variety of study methods such as birdbanding, telemetry, tracking with radar, and nighttime observation with a ceilometer which directs a powerful light into the sky. Each method has both advantages and disadvantages.

The recovery rate from birdbanding, for instance, even when performed on a large scale, is approximately 1 percent (perhaps as high as 10 percent for waterfowl). Putting a small transmitter on a bird and then tracking it with antennae and receivers placed on cars, boats, or airplanes has also yielded significant data, but it is still difficult and costly. Ceilometers are only good up to fifteen hundred feet in altitude and even then, species cannot be identified, although the numbers of migrants and their flight direction can be detected.

Radar seems to be the best bet. There are two kinds. Search radar can find large numbers of birds, and tracking radar can follow a single flock or even an individual bird. Radar can thus reveal the timing, height, direction, speed, and density of bird migration, but it cannot identify the bird species involved. To do that, old-fashioned binoculars and on-the-ground observations are necessary.

Two researchers, Janet and Timothy Williams, used radar for many years to assist them in their ongoing study of bird migration. They discovered that some members of species that migrate from North to South America—shorebirds, warblers, sparrows, and ducks—prefer to fly over water. This route takes them from Halifax (Nova Scotia), Cape Cod, or Wallops Island (Virginia) south or southeast over Bermuda and beyond. They continue southeast until they reach the Sargasso Sea. There they make use of the strong easterly trade winds that blow them back toward the Caribbean and South America. With the help of NASA radar operators at various sites, along with data collected from ships on the migration route, the Williams estimated that it takes birds just eighty hours to fly from Halifax to the Caribbean (2,000 miles); it takes another eight to twenty hours to fly on to Venezuela. They also determined the approximate altitude at which the birds flew over different areas: eight thousand feet above Bermuda, twenty thousand over Antigua, ten thousand above Barbados. By the time the birds reached Tobago, just off the South American coast, they were down to less than a thousand feet.

Species identification remained haphazard. The Williams visited selected islands during migration to see what birds had landed to feed and rest. They also traveled on ships to identify the exhausted birds, many of which died, that came down on decks. The couple even caught glimpses through binoculars of birds flying overhead. They concluded that millions of migrating birds take the Atlantic route each fall. Of those, they identified shorebirds—plovers (semipalmated, American golden, and black-bellied), ruddy turnstones, red knots, whimbrels, least and semipalmated sandpipers, Hudsonian godwits and sanderlings; songbirds—barn swallows, prothonotary and blackpoll warblers, northern waterthrushes, American redstarts, and bobolinks; raptors—ospreys and peregrine falcons; and waterfowl—green-winged and blue-winged teals.

Despite such long-distance migrators, though, estimates are that more than half of all neotropical migrants (those that winter south of the border) are heading for Mexico, the Bahamas, Cuba, and Hispaniola. Of the migrants I watched today, the rufous-sided towhees and white-throated sparrows spend their winters in the southern United States and the rest—solitary vireos, ruby-crowned kinglets, black-throated green, and Nashville warblers—are mostly neotropical migrants. The black-throated greens could go as far south as Colombia, while Nashvilles range down to Honduras, and solitary vireos may fly to Nicaragua and Cuba. Wherever they are headed, I wished them well.

OCTOBER 7. In October the woods rustle with the sounds of scurrying chipmunks gathering in their winter stores. Today I watched a small chipmunk run in its jerky way as if being pulled along on a string by a small child, its burnished red bottom gleaming in the sun. When I walked on, it froze atop a log, looking, to the uninitiated, like a tree knob that belonged there. It only popped over the edge when I took a couple more steps. Now you see them; now you don't. Like magicians' rabbits, they disappear before your very eyes.

But when I sit motionless at the base of a tree, they will often come close to peer at me. They sit up on their hindquarters, watching for the slightest movement and if, after intense scrutiny, I show no flicker of life, they resume their work and play, quite literally at my feet and once right over them.

The other day two chipmunks came racing up beside me. One took a flying leap onto the tree trunk a few inches from my outstretched legs and paused to examine me for a few minutes before resuming its game of tag. This morning, a chipmunk busily hunted for food near my feet. Suddenly a larger one dashed up, chased the smaller one away, climbed on top of a nearby stone pile and began scolding. I counted more than one thousand "chips" given without a pause before it finally disappeared into its hole.

I suspected that the larger chipmunk was the mother of the unwary smaller one because her warning call to it was so strident. At this time of year a female chipmunk who had not bred until June would still have her young ones in her care. Too young to build their own dens for the winter, they would expect to spend the cold months sharing their mother's food and den.

Digging a den is an arduous task, but the den is expected to last for a lifetime—approximately four years. They begin by digging straight down for five inches in soft soil. Then they continue at an angle for three feet, twisting and turning the two-inch-diameter shaft around rocks and tree roots. Eventually it may reach thirty feet in length with a number of offshoot tunnels, six rooms, and four or five hidden entrances. Only weasels are able to penetrate such a stronghold. The den has its own foot-square sleeping area which is filled with shredded, dry leaves and grasses. Some of their food is stored under the leaf pile while the excess is put in a nearby room.

In November or December, chipmunks settle down for their hibernationlike sleep after plugging up all the entrances with dirt. Curled in a ball, their breathing and heartbeat slow down and their body temperature drops to the level in the den. Unlike the woodchuck, though, they do not live on their fat during the long sleep. Instead, they wake up occasionally to eat from their food pile before settling back into hibernation. If they run out of food, as sometimes happens, before winter is over, they will even leave their den to gather more.

Biologists have been studying circadian rhythms in various creatures. The cycles are usually daily, monthly, or seasonal. Chipmunks, however, follow a yearly cycle. The period of inactivity that begins in November usually lasts until March—89 to 128 days—and is based on the amount of light the chipmunks are exposed to. Too much or too little light, under laboratory conditions, causes them to lose their yearly activity clock. By early March here on the mountain chipmunks will be up and around again. In April the majority of them are busy courting, and shortly afterward the females have their litters of from two to five in the same dens where they spent the winter.

Chipmunks are not strictly vegetarians, although their stored food consists of nuts, acorns, and seeds. They also get into trouble with humans for eating such delicacies as cultivated berries and cherries and the bulbs of crocuses and tulips. But they compensate for that by consuming June bugs, cutworms, and wireworms. In fact, one observer was delighted to learn that his chipmunks even enjoyed elm span worms and gypsy moths.

I often watch chipmunks fill their cheek pouches with sunflower seeds from my bird feeder in early autumn. Apparently, they are insatiable animals who will carry away all the food they can get. The famous nineteenth-century naturalist, John Burroughs, wondered if chipmunks were *ever* satisfied. One day he watched one chipmunk repeatedly stuff its cheek pouches full of food that he offered it and then carry it off to its den. It took five quarts of hickory nuts, two quarts of chestnuts, and one bushel of shelled corn before it refused any more food. Estimates by other researchers indicate that one chipmunk stores an average of eight quarts of nuts, acorns, and seeds for the winter. It takes a heap of storing to get a chipmunk through the winter.

OCTOBER 8. Thirty-four degrees at dawn, clear, rosy-fingered, with patches of frost on the lawn. A brilliant sunrise that lit up the gold of the grapevines and the wine red of the staghorn sumacs on Sapsucker Ridge called me out early, despite the frosty air. I had meant to take a short walk, but as I ascended First Field Trail, I heard the distant sound of crows mobbing something. Expecting to find a beleaguered owl, I started to follow the ear-splitting noise. Eventually, it led me to the middle of the Far Field Road.

I peered down the slope and watched as an occasional black body zeroed in on a large, thickly leaved tree. Unfortunately, the foliage was so dense that I was unable to see what was exciting the crows. The din was terrific, and nothing else could be heard above it, including my own footsteps. Directly below me, three deer wandered along, placidly feeding on the low-growing shrubs. They seemed oblivious to the noisy crows and to my presence as well.

A movement on the trail ahead of me made me ease my binoculars up to my eyes in time to spot a red fox picking its way slowly toward me. As I watched, it veered off down the slope in the direction of the crow noise which, after a few minutes, rose to an even louder crescendo.

Then they abruptly dispersed. My ears rang in the unaccustomed silence, and slowly I turned away. This time the deer heard me and fled. Once more I was only a disruptive force in the forest. Yet because of the crow noise, I had been able, for a short time, to watch the flow of forest life without the creatures knowing I was abroad.

OCTOBER 9. Still another clear, breezy, warming day, aiding and abetting the destruction of the forest by the lumberman's team of three men, who are ably assisted by the screeching, earth-crushing skidders, a massive bulldozer, and a couple of chain saws. Do those men feel mighty when they fell the giants or are they merely doing a job?

At midday I fled once more to the peace and serenity of the Far Field, trying to appreciate the beauty of this saddest of all seasons. The warm afternoon belonged chiefly to chasing chipmunks and buzzing flies revitalized by the sunshine. Gray squirrels scolded at my silent presence, and a flock of singing, calling birds—tufted titmice, black-capped chickadees, a solitary vireo, and unidentifiable chips and trills—performed somewhere high in the treetops behind where I was sitting.

Is it blasphemy to paraphrase the Bible and think that the Far Field is my refuge and my strength, a very present help in the time of need? For so I think of it and my need to flee there, as trees crash to the ground over and over, the sounds reverberating throughout the walls of our house. The Far Field is my balm of Gilead, and when I finally stood up to walk on, two wild turkeys ran off from the edge of the field. All those rustling noises I had been hearing had not been dry leaves blown down by the wind, but turkeys moving slowly toward me. Once again, sitting at the base of the same wild black cherry tree had brought me luck—last time a gray fox, today two wild turkeys.

OCTOBER 10. I found another wonderful old cherry tree to sit against late this afternoon. I grow more and more fond of the species. For sheer comfort as a backrest in the woods, mature cherry trees can't be beat. I settled down in an area of mostly large oak and pignut hickory trees. The latter were festooned with a thick growth of grapevines which are attractive to wildlife.

Chipmunks rustled in the leaves with their usual ebullience, but what caught my interest were the gray squirrels silently toting hickory nuts down one tree and off into a cache somewhere nearby. In contrast to the chipmunks, the squirrels seemed grave, quiet, and highly businesslike in their demeanor. Then I spotted two youngsters about halfway up the hickory tree. They were slowly circling the tree trunk while a larger squirrel, probably their mother, headed down the tree with a nut in her mouth, ignoring the two smaller ones. They leaped into a tangle of grape-vines that hung from the tree branches about twenty feet above the ground and began frolicking. Slowly I sat down and trained my binoculars on them. My movement caught their attention, and for a few seconds they paused to scru-tinize me. But I remained still, so they soon ignored me.

For the most part their play was silent. I only heard three muffled squeaks in the hour I sat there. They fre-quently patted each other's faces, nuzzled each other's tails and played "follow the leader" through the grapevines. Often they would cling together on a drooping vine, chest to chest, one squirrel with its head facing upward and the other with its head down. Then, still in that position, they would wrap their front legs around each other. They seemed to use their front legs just as we use arms. One squirrel would grasp the other from behind, looking for all the world as if it were hugging its sibling around the waist. They also paused occasionally to sit up like minia-ture boxers and feint with their paws, which remained open instead of clenched. They were never far apart. If one went ahead of the other, it would pause and wait until its partner caught up before proceeding. As I watched I became more entranced. Those squirrels seemed to ex-hibit a caring, almost loving attitude toward each other, something I had never observed so clearly before in wild animals. I have read books by people who have been close to wild animals and who have written about the very qual-ities I was observing. But it is one thing to read about it and another to see it for myself.

Not long ago, attributing humanlike attitudes to wild creatures was disdainfully called anthropomorphism by cooler scientific minds. Yet, as more and more field studies of mammals are conducted by biologists, such views are no longer scoffed at, although there is no agreement about the level of intensity of animal emotions. Most people believe that wild animals do not have feelings toward each other that are as strong as those of humans. On the other hand, the growing "animal rights" movement is based, in part, in the belief that animals, both domesticated and wild, have feelings as refined as ours, and for that reason should not be used in scientific experiments to test the safety of our cosmetics, pesticides, and drugs, or be killed to provide us with furs and food.

The more I watch the wildlife of our mountain, the less certain I am that animals are much different than we are in their emotions. Maybe nature's scheme is less ordered and more emotional than we think. Could love be a cohesive force among all members of the order *Mammalia,* just as it is among *Homo sapiens?* On the other hand, there is no denying the old saying, "Nature red in tooth and claw," so while I personally am not a hunter, I am also not a strict vegetarian. Like most humans, I compromise in order to live in what is sometimes a cruel, sometimes a marvelous natural world. "To do no harm" is probably an impossible goal for humans, yet it is one that we can all strive toward, taking only what we *need* to live, reining in our greed for more by always asking first, "At what price? Who or what will suffer?" The Native Americans' custom of asking permission of a creature to take its life as well as begging its forgiveness afterward is the kind of reverence for life that humans should strive for—to look on nature's gifts as a privilege, not a right.

With such an approach, the needless killing of both animals and humans, the wasteful slaughtering of forests, the fouling of water, air, and soil would not be occurring. They are a byproduct of "progress," which is supposed to improve our lives, but the truth is that the quality of our lives is steadily declining and the profit from all this plunder principally lines the pockets of the rich. It is for their benefit that we forfeit our birthright, having sold the earth for a mess of pottage long ago.

OCTOBER 11. Damp and overcast this morning, but it seems unable to rain anymore. We had a few spits late yesterday afternoon, not even enough to wet the concrete walkway below the back steps.

I walked down the hollow road this morning to check on the lumbering. I heard at least two chain saws, one further down the hollow than the other, and the steady crashing of enormous trees. It took less than a minute to fell one. Deer grazed calmly on the remnants of Margaret's lawn, chipmunks chased above the road, birds continually called, leaves rained down. All nature seemed undisturbed by the noise, or perhaps merely resigned to it.

I am *not* resigned. Each falling tree pierced me to the bone, and nowhere on the mountain could I find peace. The roar of skidders and chain saws overwhelmed me until I reached the Far Field Road where the din faded. But the sounds of motors and machines came up clearly from Sinking Valley. Even at the Far Field, noise from the highway and more distant chain sawing intruded—cars honked, trains whistled—there is no more silence on earth, and few people seem to notice. In fact, most are uncomfortable when faced with quiet. It means they must entertain themselves instead of being entertained—read, walk, think, contemplate. But these will soon be lost arts, overwhelmed by the allure of noisy technology in the form of all-terrain vehicles, television, boom-boxes, VCRs. Such bread and circuses distract people from thinking and observing and possibly becoming discontent with our violent, intrusive, consumer-oriented society. They might begin to wonder if life isn't more than the mindless consumption of goods and entertainment to raise the illusory Gross National Product. It seems as if monasteries and convents should be coming back into favor soon, because, as in the tumultuous Middle Ages, they offer a haven from societal upheavals.

I returned along the First Field Trail, still accompanied by the lumbering cacophony, but I discovered the woods were alive with birds—yellow-rumped warblers by the hundreds, golden-crowned kinglets, solitary vireos, tufted titmice, and black-capped chickadees, with occasionally the "look-at-me" song of a ruby-crowned kinglet. Finally I sat down, willing to be seduced by the charm of the fluttering yellow-rumps. They flew in close, as fearless as golden-crowned kinglets. For long, wonderful moments I was surrounded by them, several in each tree, and when I walked on after that flock had moved up the mountaintop, I met another flock. Truly it was a day for yellow-rumped warblers—immatures, females, males— each with a different color scheme, but all sporting the yellow tail spot that flashed as they foraged.

Later, after the lumbermen had roared off for the day, I sat on the veranda to drink a cup of tea in the sudden quiet and spotted a white creature walking down the field beside the barn. It was a striped skunk—black-faced with a white stripe down the middle, a black belly and legs, a buffy beige back, and mostly snow white tail. It waddled about, digging its nose into the weeds as I watched through binoculars. Then it disappeared into a patch of dried goldenrod beside the corn crib.

Cautiously I walked down near the bend in the driveway and spotted it again in the tall grasses. Occasionally it made small lunges with its head and front paws as it hunted grasshoppers. Then I was temporarily sidetracked by the call of a pine siskin. In that moment of inattention, the skunk disappeared from sight, and I hadn't the courage to follow it into the long field grasses. With skunks, it is better to know precisely where they are before following them.

In the evening Bruce spotted the skunk foraging on the guesthouse lawn. It scuttled under a white lilac bush, and from the road, slightly less than the prerequisite ten feet to avoid the spray if the skunk were so inclined, Bruce had a look at it in the gathering dusk. After watching him nervously, the skunk retreated down the bank to the stream. We agreed that its overall white top made it an unusually beautiful skunk, although I later read that the blacker the skunk, the more its pelt is prized by trappers.

OCTOBER 12. A slow, gray dawn, but a crow cawed, a white-throated sparrow sang, and gray squirrels made merry on the lawn.

I walked down the hollow road, savoring the weekend peace now that the loggers are gone for a couple of days. A winter wren bounced up and called at the bridge, chipmunks "chipped" as they dashed along the almost dry streambed which they are using now as a highway, leaping over the occasional puddles—all that remains of our hollow stream during the prolonged drought.

From where I later sat, slightly above the road on the lumberman's property, the hollow looked unchanged, and except for an occasional airplane it was free of humanity's noise. The woods were redolent of fallen autumn leaves, that wonderful odor which distinguishes the season to those of us who love the woods.

A fox squirrel sat phlegmatically in the road eating a nut. Then it leaped slowly off into the woods as I watched. Only a fringe of trees was left on the lumberman's property above the road as I walked further down the hollow. Otherwise, I saw open sky as I looked up the slope. At the bottom of the mountain I spotted a patch of blue sky over the town, and in little over ten minutes the sun came out and lit the woods in all its autumnal glory. A silent wood thrush flushed beside the stream. The birds reactivated in the warm light—solitary vireos, white-throated sparrows, and ruby-crowned kinglets sang while the black-capped chickadees, tufted titmice, pileated and hairy woodpeckers, yellow-rumped warblers, and golden-crowned kinglets contented themselves with calls. Later, a breeze sent leaves spinning down as I lay above the first pulloff in an old hole made by an uprooted tree. I felt at home, surrounded by birds high in the treetops, pelted by falling leaves and warmed by an intermittent sun lately risen above Laurel Ridge.

Finally, I walked up the second side hollow to the lumberman's Lower Road, treading on a path of fallen golden and scarlet red maple leaves and scaring off a perched red-tailed hawk which silently spiraled upward into the sky. The red maples continued on up the hollow, lighting up the woods from within. At the untouched third side hollow a Carolina wren sang, accompanied by a winter wren, three northern flickers, an American robin, dark-eyed juncos, white-throated sparrows, tufted titmice, and a pileated woodpecker.

As I reluctantly braced myself to face what lay ahead, the overcast skies returned and the brief moments of sunshine were gone. The Upper Road had been scraped clean of every piece of vegetation; if this isn't a clear-cut, I don't know what is. Amid the downed trees I spotted a fox squirrel, probably the same one I had watched back in August when its world was still intact. It sat frozen in place, halfway up a small, gnarled tree, worthless to the lumbermen and therefore uncut. Around it lay total devastation—a treeless knoll strewn with still green branches. A fruity smell emanated from a broken witch hazel shrub still bravely blossoming even though it was slashed and dying. An innocent victim, as were all the little shrubs and trees—"trash trees" in the parlance of foresters—not only witch hazel, but flowering dogwood and red maples, crushed when the big ones fell. So much for all the assurances we had heard from the lumberman and his forester for over four years about what an excellent job they would do. How often had they told us that they would never do a clear-cut—only butchers did that?

Suddenly, over the silence of destruction, the church chimes from town began their noon concert for the faithful, reminding me that our lumberman neighbor once told us that he believed God put trees on the earth for humans to harvest just like fields of corn. Well, his God is not my God. And increasingly, theologians are distressed by the attitude, still prevalent in many fundamentalist Christian circles, which is based on the words of Genesis: "Be fruitful and multiply, and replenish the Earth and subdue it: and have dominion over the fish of the sea and over the fowl of the air and over every living thing that moveth upon the earth."

One churchman, Lynn White, Jr., in his famous essay "The Historical Roots of Our Ecologic Crisis," argues that our Western culture's enthrallment with science and technology is "deeply conditioned" by religion. Christianity, he claims, is "the most anthropocentric religion the world has seen," because it believes that "God planned all of this explicitly for man's benefit and rule: no item in the physical creation had any purpose save to serve man's purposes" (p. 1205). White hopes that this doctrine of human dominance over nature will change to a belief in "the democracy of all God's creatures," and that Christians will adopt the ideals of St. Francis in a reformed Christianity (p. 1206). His call to reform "awakened many of us from our doldrums," James A. Nash writes in his definitive and encouraging (to Christian environmentalists) book

Loving Nature: Ecological Integrity and Christian Responsibility (p. 71). He finds, in the Bible, ample justification for St. Francis's reverence for life. Nash extends the doctrine of Christian love to all God's creatures, by allowing them the right to live free, unfettered lives in proper ecological niches that have not been denuded by humanity. Furthermore, Nash devises a "Bill of Biotic Rights" which, if adopted by Christians everywhere, would lead to a more sustainable culture based on harmony between humans and nature replacing the present doctrine of human competition and greed that the unsustainable cutting of forests represents.

To me, our lumberman neighbor is like one of the greedy moneychangers that Christ drove from the temple. But he sees himself as a canny businessman making the kind of profits our society admires, based on an interpretation of the Bible that threatens to destroy the earth. He believes that humans have dominion over the earth, so he does not hesitate to bend nature to his will. To him and others of his ilk, a managed world is a beautiful world. Wilderness must be beaten back and subdued in order that humans can thrive. Those of us who protest are impeding progress, humanity's steady march toward prosperity. Why then is there less and less as we slash and burn our way across the planet?

OCTOBER 13. The steep skid road gouged deeply into the mountainside by an earlier lumberman, before we could purchase the land, has allowed me to take long, strenuous circular walks—down the road, up the mountainside, and back along Laurel Ridge. For the first couple of years I did this infrequently because the lumbering scars were too fresh. But lately, the scars have begun to soften, and climbing the skid road has become my test to see if I am still in shape. Still, I had not been up it for a year and a half. Today, this on-and-off, sunny-cloudy, brisk autumn weather tempted me to test my mettle once again.

I found the road so overgrown with grass, goldenrod, white wood asters, ferns, white snakeroot, Pennsylvania smartweed, striped maple saplings, and Hercules' club that it was difficult, in some places, to figure out which direction it went. The higher I climbed, the better the road looked. This, after all, had not been a clear-cut. Many excellent seed trees of every species had been left, and much of the understory had survived. In one open area along the road, a maze of chestnut and red oak seedlings were interspersed with bracken ferns, blueberry shrubs, and mountain laurel. They had even left most of the red oak trees on a moss-covered knoll. Finally, I reached the top of the steepest slope to be met by a forest of scarlet gleaming in the sunlight—a large grove of understory black gum trees twenty to thirty feet high at their pinnacle of brilliance. Beneath them I found several two-leaved, red maple seedlings which had turned a pure purplish blue such as I had never seen before.

Once I had thought what this lumberman had done with his bulldozer and skidder had been the worst that could happen. But now that our neighbor has started his operation with the services of a young forester fresh from the university, I realized that Margaret had been right. "Never trust a lumberman." Especially not one with pretensions to do the right thing. I stood recalling the conversation I had had with his forester when they first bulldozed out the Upper and Lower Roads.

"Will your job look better than the one at the end of the mountain?" I asked him. A look of scorn crossed his face.

"That was a butcher's job," he said. "We wouldn't think of doing anything that bad. My boss cares about the land, otherwise, he wouldn't hire a forester." To be fair, the forester no longer works full time for the lumberman. In fact, I am convinced that he has had nothing to do with the current job, which looks more and more like the work of a man desperate for money.

OCTOBER 14. I first heard the strange call eleven and a half years ago. I had been sitting in the Far Field thicket for an hour or more, watching large snowflakes drift slowly down around me, when the silence was broken by low, grumbling noises coming from somewhere in the treetops.

"Strange crow," I thought as I glimpsed a large black bird flapping slowly away. "Sounded like it had a cold." And for a time I believed that the noisemaker had been an aberrant American crow. But as I heard it more and more often on the road to the Far Field, at the Far Field itself, and in the thicket, I became suspicious.

First of all, there were two birds instead of one. Crows, I knew, usually were either alone or in a flock. In addition, the birds were secretive and difficult to see. Never once did they give the familiar "caw-caw" cry of crows. The mystery continued for several months until the day in early spring when I sat at the pond watching wood frogs. Two large black birds flew over First Field, circled above Margaret's home and then returned, all the while making the peculiar calls of my mysterious thicket birds.

For once I had a good look at them out in the open. As I watched, a mob of crows suddenly appeared on the scene. They were smaller than the mystery birds, which did not prevent the crows from chasing them. At last I knew what they were. A pair of common ravens had come to live on our mountain. A few days later Margaret called to tell me about the strange crows that were walking majestically around her yard.

"They act like they own the place," she reported. "They walk right up to the house even when the dog is out."

"They are not crows," I said. "They're ravens." Immediately what had previously been to her common, pesky birds became glamorous new birds to watch and admire. However, despite her championship of them, most of her visitors insisted they were nothing but "old crows." But Margaret checked the field characteristics as I gave them to her. First of all, the ravens were nearly twice the bulk of crows. They also had shaggy throat feathers which she could see when they perched nearby. Their tails were large and wedge-shaped, and they alternated flapping with soaring on horizontal wings instead of soaring with their wings bent upward like crows. Furthermore, they croaked instead of cawed.

The ravens hung around Margaret's place for weeks and even charged visitors when they came near a wooded area above her home. They probably had built their nest in the highest evergreen tree, a favorite nesting habitat for Pennsylvania's common ravens. Those tree nests are huge structures—four feet or more across—but because they are so high in the treetops, they are well concealed from the ground, making them almost impossible to locate. Ravens prefer to line their nests with bark shreds and deer hair, in particular their white belly hair mixed with some red hair from their backs. All this they gather from dead deer—they are, by and large, scavengers in their eating habits.

The female lays two to seven eggs and incubates them for three weeks while the male stands guard. Then both birds take care of the young during their four weeks in the nest and for several weeks more once they fledge. Eventually, though, the young leave to establish their own territories; individual pairs are solitary creatures and do not like to live close to other ravens. Scientists think that ravens mate for life, and certainly I have rarely seen one without the other on our mountain. They prefer wild, rocky mountaintops far from humans both for living and nesting.

In *The American Crow and the Common Raven,* Lawrence Kilham wrote: "To get at the mind of a crow is a great challenge, but to get at the mind of a raven . . . is an even greater one. Ravens are, to enthusiasts like myself, at the top of the avian pyramid in mental attributes" (p. 186). On his New Hampshire farm, he baited in both crows and ravens with food, using cow and lamb carcasses and suet, and quickly discovered that ravens enjoyed waylaying and robbing crows of food when they flew off with it in their bills. A pair of ravens were enough to keep seventy-seven crows upset and outmaneuvered in both the woods and in the open. Crows, it seemed, did the dirty, dangerous work of landing and feeding on carcasses while the ravens hung back or were extremely wary when they did land, using the crows as sentinels. On the other hand, common ravens are bold in robbing birds' nests of both eggs and young, and Kilham observed one fly off with a large common grackle nestling in its bill. The crows often mobbed ravens, since ravens enjoy young crows as well as other young birds in their diet.

But Kilham and many other observers of common ravens have also noted what appears to be a fondness for play, especially in the air. This autumn day I watched a pair of ravens tumbling in the wind and sunlight above Sapsucker Ridge. They executed loop-de-loops, flying into the wind, wings swept back, matching each other stroke for stroke, all the while rending the air with their strange, wild cries. It was a sight of sheer exuberance that I will remember a long time—common ravens on fall winds, lifting my spirits to an autumnal high despite the distant sounds of chain saws down the ridge.

OCTOBER 15. Raining hard most of the morning, which drove the loggers from the hollow for the first time. Then a brisk wind picked up, clearing the skies and sending a mosaic of colored leaves to the ground. When I walked the trails in early afternoon, I felt like a medieval queen treading on a sinuous cloth of gold.

From the top of First Field, the view, with its alternate light and shade flickering against the symphony of color, inspires awe. On such a day I feel as if no other place on earth could be as beautiful as our piece of the Appalachian Mountains. They may be incredibly old and worn down, but they are verdant, proof that old age needn't be ugly or deprived but expansive and breathtaking. To go out with your flame still burning, like the leaves of autumn, is the way to die, but are we reborn as the trees are each spring?

From 3:30 until 5:00 I joined Steve at the top of First Field to watch the raptor migration. It remained windy with some wispy clouds, and he continued to adjust his scope and help me zero in on the raptors which were sometimes so high in the sky that all I could see with my naked eyes was the shape of the wings and a flash of white before they rose out of sight, gone into the infinite blue which seemed to dissolve them. But in that short time Steve showed me one northern harrier, two sharp-shinned hawks, one Cooper's hawk, five turkey vultures, twenty-three red-tailed hawks, three killdeer, a flock of blackbirds, nine American crows, and, our best sighting, one osprey flying directly overhead. Everyone should lie on a promontory on a windy October day, scanning for raptors and spinning with the earth. It cleanses the soul.

OCTOBER 16. Dawn comes later now. When I went downstairs to fix breakfast this morning I walked across a sitting room still illuminated by moonlight. Venus, the "morning star," shone brightly in the lightening sky as Sirius moved west to make way for the sun. By the time Bruce left for work, the birds were stirring in the half-light and three does leapt off from the lawn, bounding up into the field with many a backward glance.

First a song sparrow sang his cheery song. Then a white-throated sparrow rendered a rusty version of his mournful "poor Sam Peabody, Peabody, Peabody" call. Just after the seven o'clock factory whistle sounded from town, a rufous-sided towhee "chewinked," closely followed by the "yanking" of two questing white-breasted nuthatches on the balm-of-Gilead tree and the "mew" of a gray catbird in the lilac bush beside the front porch.

An eastern screech owl called faintly from the ridge while the eastern phoebe, who sings louder each day, reminded me he is still in residence. Tufted titmice streamed back from the deep woods where they had spent the summer, scolding and hinting that it would be nice if I put the bird feeder up.

As the sunlight touched Sapsucker Ridge, the first American crow cawed, followed immediately by blue jays in full voice. Then a pileated woodpecker trumpeted loudly as it began its day in the ridge trees. Suddenly our unlit yard trees were alive with birds. The silent ones were eastern bluebirds peering into their old nest box, the holes in the black walnut tree, and those in the balm-of-Gilead. Whether they were contemplating winter quarters or merely checking out next spring's nesting possibilities, I don't know.

Many of the flitting birds high in the trees were fall warblers, and my eyes were not quick enough in the dim light to sort them out. But one gave himself away. "Witchedy, witchedy, witchedy," he called, and I wrote down "common yellowthroat" on my list. A flock of northern flickers flew past. Their wings flashed gold beneath, identifying them as members of the yellow-shafted race. American robins "tut-tutted" from the tallest trees, and a female downy woodpecker gleaned insects from the balm-of-Gilead near the back porch as I stood looking over the grapevines and blackberry canes pulsating with bird life.

One bird—close in, nondescript, pumping its tail vigorously as it occupied a berry bush—caught my attention. It was another one of those confusing fall warblers, and I tried to ignore it. But unlike most warblers, it stayed near and relatively still except for its incessantly bobbing tail. I concentrated on the tail and noticed a spot of yellow beneath its base. It couldn't be a yellow-rumped warbler because that bird is named for the yellow above its tail base. But when I checked my Peterson bird guide under "yellow-rumped," I was rewarded. Right beside it was the bird I had watched. "Brownish back, yellowish undertail coverts. Bobs tail," Peterson wrote. Our yard had been visited this morning by a palm warbler that had spent its summer in muskeg and sphagnum moss country and was heading south for its winter among the palms of the southern Atlantic coast. The identification of a confusing fall warbler gave me a sense of triumph that stayed with me during what turned out to be a very "birdy" day.

Later, on my walk, I detonated ruffed grouse as I moved along the trails and almost, but not quite, caught the one on the Guesthouse Trail drumming on his log. Seven dark-eyed juncos flew up from the edge of First Field at the beginning of the Short Circuit Trail. Suddenly warblers were everywhere, foraging around me like fluttering butterflies. I sat down and "pished," attracting one male black-throated green warbler, dozens of yellow-rumped warblers, and two solitary vireos, one of which sang for me. Dark-eyed juncos and black-capped chickadees also hovered around. Even a downy woodpecker alighted beside me. This was one of those magic times when birds forage and flutter, plucking large caterpillars from leaves and unseen insects from limbs and trunks, without paying any attention to me as I sat cross-legged, binoculars swinging from one hovering bird to another. The spectacle lasted for over fifteen minutes and then, in an instant it seemed, the trees around me emptied out.

Lying up in First Field in mid-afternoon under a clear, blue sky, warmed by the sun and surrounded by dried goldenrod and singing insects, I watched spiders spinning webs, looking as if they were pirouetting in space, defying nature, without anchorage to any solid base. Through half-closed eyes I could see monarch butterflies floating past.

When I finally stood up and walked down from the field, I heard an unfamiliar song, but all I could find were foraging song sparrows. After the singing stopped. I spotted a white-crowned sparrow sitting silently in a Norway spruce tree. It remained fully visible and looked around for at least five minutes before it flew off. Then, at the base of the powerline right-of-way, I discovered a large flock of mixed sparrows—field, song, white-throated, and at least ten white-crowned sparrows. Never before had I seen so many white-crowned sparrows on our mountaintop.

OCTOBER 17. Overcast but with a high cloud cover so the views are still clear. The second thicket rustled with birds and reverberated with songs and calls—rufous-sided towhees, white-throated sparrows, northern cardinals, a winter wren, tufted titmice, American robins, a pair of hermit thrushes, and another pair of northern flickers. The longer I sat there, the closer the birds came. First the pair of hermit thrushes, their tails flicking, landed within ten feet of me low in the spicebushes. Next, the flickers moved in to feed on wild grapes. Then I watched one hermit thrush as it ran along a log and the ground like a robin, head thrust forward, taking several running steps at a time.

But a gray squirrel leaped from another tree. The thrush flew off while the squirrel continued toward me, finally stopping four feet away in a gnarled dead tree overhung with grapes. It eyed me warily and made a low, grumbly noise deep in its throat, almost like a cat's purring, before running on up the tree. A second squirrel hopped up, scolded me loudly and agitated its tail, but I clicked my tongue back at it, keeping up a dialogue for a minute or two before it fled back into the brush.

Finally, I was too cold to continue sitting, so I walked on over to the hunting lodge property, determined to explore their upper trail. The property is large and was once a farm; the weathered old house still stands, along with a barn and the much-used outhouse. The owners, a group of hunting buddies and their families, manage the place as a hunting preserve, with wide jeep trails and a series of fields cultivated and planted in corn or grass. There is a pond below the house which they put in years ago, but I never find much sign of life in or around it, maybe because the grounds are kept so well mown that there is no cover for animals nearby.

The upper trail—an old woods road—runs along the top of Sapsucker Ridge, and I surprised a foraging wild turkey that had just trotted up from the heavily wooded slope toward the highway. Despite the gray white day, the woods were a blur of wonderful color—mostly young red maple trees. A line of huge red oak trees on the highway side of the upper trail marked the property boundary with a valley neighbor who does not manage the land. Here is one of the few places on the mountain where there are substantial groves of white birch trees. Those, along with the brilliant maple color, made me think I was in Vermont instead of Pennsylvania.

I started musing on how much I would love to own this property because it is large and relatively flat. Even though the woods are young, the red maples are abundant and beautiful. But suddenly I realized why this land looks so different from ours, and why it does not rustle with wildlife. There are no wild grapevines festooning trees, and no real food for wild creatures. While the neatness is aesthetically pleasing to that part of me that loves order, in comparison to our own uncut, unmanaged land, replete with weeds in the fields and grapevines in the woods, it is not productive in terms of biological diversity and attractiveness to wildlife.

Although I did pass black birch trees with cones that had attracted several yellow-rumped warblers, and I finally flushed three deer where a thicket of striped maples formed a small understory, for the most part I saw little but wide vistas and neat borders. At last I came out at the top of their manicured fields and had a breathtaking view of the red maple woods beyond—a palette of colors even more striking because of the white sky in the background.

Shortly after noon, I heard, as I sat quietly contemplating the color, the sound of Canada geese calling. A straight line of seventy-two flew overhead, pointed south across the valley. I felt overawed, as if I had been led to this remote spot to bear witness to the presence of geese passing over the autumnal landscape. With nothing but my feet, I could walk a few miles into adventure and wildness and beauty; in just a few hours I was rewarded with so many new sights and thoughts. Because the more I walked those neat acres, the more I realized what else was missing. There was no underbrush in most places, no dead trees, hence no woodpeckers, no ferns, no dried goldenrod, or any other dried weed flowers in the fields.

In their mania for neatness, they have ordered nature like a European deer park and so have limited wildlife and plants. The food that is there for wildlife is mostly food that they have planted themselves—cultivated corn and a hedge of autumn olive loaded with berries. They must have read every wildlife management book and listened to every forester about "weed trees" and "strangler" grapes and "trashy" Hercules club. So, this is not wildness at all, this is humanity at its controlling best, certain that its ways can improve on nature's. Hence, I saw no grouse, few deer, one lone turkey that had wandered up from the wild acres below, very few songbirds, no evidence of foxes, squirrels, chipmunks, or woodchucks, no den holes in the field—a pretty, well-cared-for, green desert.

When I crossed back to our unkempt land, wildlife reappeared and the woods rustled once again with chipmunks, gray squirrels, and ruffed grouse and reverberated with the calls of woodpeckers. At the Far Field thicket I stopped to watch a mixed flock of singing ruby-crowned kinglets and white-throated sparrows. The kinglets twirled like hummingbirds, their wings whirling, their beaks probing into the last of the fading field asters.

I wished I could tell the well-meaning hunters who own the hunting camp, "Don't manage it. Nature will do a better job and you will have both more huntable wildlife and more biological diversity if you leave it alone." But, like humanity everywhere, they believe that if they don't fiddle with it, it will self-destruct. The image of humans as stewards of the land should relinquish its place to humans as watchers. In the meantime, as all the landowners around us "manage" their land by cutting their mature trees and tearing down their wild grapevines, the hunters swarm over our property, realizing that even though it looks messy with all those weeds and grapevines and dead trees, it is a paradise for grouse and turkeys and deer, not to mention foxes and squirrels and woodchucks.

OCTOBER 18. A purple sky with Jupiter and Venus nestled close together, still shining as the night brightened into day. The morning sky was a deep blue, and I sat at the

base of a huge red oak tree above the Far Field Road, surrounded by light and color. Enough leaves have fallen that
the ground gleamed with as many shades of red, orange,
and gold as the trees. Surely this is the most beautiful autumn we have ever had here.

Beside the Far Field Trail I spotted a foraging buck before he spotted me, and so I was able to get a good, close
look before he suddenly glanced up, turned, and galloped
off. Bucks are so much heavier and less graceful than does.
They run differently, with a sense of perceived majesty,
and are more alert. This one had a small, two-point rack,
a young buck I imagine. My rule of thumb, even when
there are no antlers to give them away, is that a deer alone
is a buck. The does are more sociable and like a crowd,
although occasionally I have found two bucks together.

Along Laurel Ridge Trail, I watched a mixed flock of
ruby- and golden-crowned kinglets, scolding tufted titmice, and a hairy woodpecker. Cedar waxwings keened
along the powerline right-of-way. Ruffed grouse clucked
and flushed at the edge of First Field. A red-bellied woodpecker called, then an American robin, a white-breasted
nuthatch, black-capped chickadees, and eastern bluebirds.
A gray squirrel bent all its concentrated powers into gathering nuts, so it did not see me until it came within five
feet of where I was standing. Headed straight toward me
with a nut in its mouth, it paused, turned slowly around
and then hopped just as slowly up on a log and out of
sight, not appearing rushed or frightened as gray squirrels
usually do. This one seemed to be a gray squirrel with a
fox squirrel personality.

Steve drove downtown with me in the afternoon and
was, as usual, watching the woods closely. Just below the
forks he suddenly said, "What's that white animal up in
the woods?" I stopped and peered with him halfway up
Laurel Ridge slope where we could clearly see a large

white animal—someone's hunting dog perhaps. Unfortunately we had no binoculars with us, but we did have Steve's super eyes.

"I see dark, deerlike ears on it," he said, which propelled both of us out of the car for a clearer look. I noticed a little beige on the side of its face, but otherwise it was all white. When it moved, we finally spotted its brown mother and a sibling behind it. No doubt about it, a young white deer lives in our woods, the first we have ever seen here. But white deer are so highly prized that they appear in countless place-names in Pennsylvania: White Deer Ridge, White Deer Valley, White Deer Creek, White Deer Furnace, White Deer Pike, and the community of White Deer. Few white deer survive long, though, because they are coveted by hunters seeking unique trophies, and unless we have a lasting snow soon, it will be an easy target for any trigger-happy person. Once, several years ago, I found a white woodchuck at the Far Field, but no matter how often I revisited the area, I never saw it again. I suspect the same will be true of the white deer. So we looked our fill until it wandered out of sight, and we wished it well.

OCTOBER 19. For some reason, I seem to have my closest encounters with eastern box turtles in October. Several years ago, on a hazy, warm day with a breeze that showered down a steady rain of leaves, I set out for a day in the woods, my pack on my back, ready for adventure.

On the road below the second thicket, a rustle in the leaves alerted me to the presence of a box turtle at my feet. Slowly I eased myself down beside it. Instantly, it started to retreat into its shell, but as I remained still, its head slowly reemerged, enabling me to see its fiery red eyes— the eyes, almost certainly of a male, since females usually have dark red, reddish brown, purple, or gray eyes.

I watched his throat palpitating as he stretched his wrinkled orange neck as high as it could reach—about three inches. Then he slowly turned his head toward me and studied me with those red eyes. Turtles see very well and even have keen color perception. He must have decided that I looked safe enough in my blue jeans and orange shirt because after several silent minutes spent watching me, he turned his head away and began his slow plodding walk forward through the dry, crackling leaves. Moving his clawed front feet like a swimmer doing the Australian crawl, he tackled each small incline as if it were a wave in the sea to be crested.

During the time I watched, he stopped frequently to crane his neck and look carefully about, but he never gave me a backward glance. He had probably not yet forgotten me, however, because researchers have proved that turtles have fair memories. Certainly I would never forget the close-up view I had had of him, with his horny yellow beak, orange neck, and glittering eyes. In the slow silence of the time we had together, I felt as if I had taken a small step toward bridging the yawning gap between human and reptilian perception.

Then, today, I had another close encounter with the eastern box turtle. This one—another male—had his front end up on a small limb, and he stared at me with orange red eyes through his half-opened hinge. If a box turtle can look comical, this one did. He pulled back in farther as I touched his shell; then he opened slightly again to keep an eye on me, or so it seemed.

I am convinced that box turtles have individual personalities, and I labeled this one "curious." I sat about eight feet away, dozing against a tree, consciously retreating back into turtle time. Slowly, slowly the turtle's head emerged. After many long, contemplative moments, he turned around and headed slowly through the woods, his side to me so I could observe precisely how he walked. First he lifted one front foot, then its opposite back foot, then the other front foot, and finally its opposite back foot. He held his head up very high, and his alert eyes watched everything. The bottom of his shell was elevated above the ground as he walked, just like the desert tortoise we had watched out in Utah a couple of years ago. After every few steps, he paused, sat back on his shell, looked carefully around, and then hoisted himself slowly up and plodded forward again for a few steps before again pausing, peering around, and moving on with deliberate reptilian haste. No wonder it is impossible to sneak up on a box turtle. They are more alert than birds or mammals. But then they have been around much longer, 200 million years, in fact, and have been practically unchanged over that period. In addition, they are considered the most intelligent of the reptiles. Slow, easy, smart, and cautious— those seem to be the traits that have kept them going for so long. Perhaps we should heed the lessons of the turtle and cultivate those same traits in ourselves. Certainly the heedless, fast pace of modern-day society, built on a belief in media sound bites and car bumper slogans, does not seem to be doing our mental or physical health much good, and at this point I doubt our ability to survive as a species even a fraction as long as turtles have.

OCTOBER 20. A frosty weekend morning, clear and brisk. Bruce and I walked down the road and then detoured up onto the lumberman's property to see how much more of the hollow had been cut. New roads, devoid of vegetation and deeply grooved with skidder marks, led in every direction. No longer could we refer to the Upper and Lower Roads with any kind of certitude. Many seemingly sound, large trees had been cut and then left to lie as if the cutting frenzy could not be controlled, illustrating a philosophy which seemed to be that the only good woods was a treeless woods. In fact, the lumberman had once used the phrase to Bruce, "the woods wants to be cut," as if the trees themselves have a death wish.

The contrast between the stunning autumn colors and the crushed and dying understory and piles of logs was almost unbearably poignant. White-throated sparrows called in the distance; displaced gray squirrels scolded in rumbling undertones. In one area, only a single large tree was left standing because it still had the remnants of a hunting platform attached to it. Along the Upper Road I had once counted eight hunting platforms and had lamented their dilapidated condition, their unsightly appearance, the harm all those nails and spikes were doing to the trees. How ironical that only those trees are now left standing.

I bade my final farewells to the "wilderness" knoll, since a new bulldozer track was aimed straight for it. Bruce took "before" photos, figuring, by next week, that he'll be able to take "after" photos. By then, what I thought of as the womb of the mountain will be ripped out. I sat there and "pished" in brown creepers, black-capped chickadees, tufted titmice, white-breasted nuthatches, and golden-crowned kinglets, before moving down to the Lower Road. We tried to walk back along its remains, but it was a tangle of downed trees, especially in the side hollows. Many trees were cut below the road and the supposed 200-foot limit, as if they could not bear to pass by any decent-sized tree, but still we gave them the benefit of the doubt, assuming that they hadn't measured very accurately. Above the road there are no large trees left and precious few small ones. No wonder we can now see so much blue sky from the hollow road. The forest is gone.

I sat outside all afternoon, drinking in the peace of Sunday and mentally preparing myself for the ravaging weeks ahead until the hollow is stripped. Three deer grazed on the lawn as I read, one less than ten feet away. Later, as I made dinner, I looked down into the flat area and watched a doe licking and licking, first one youngster, then the other.

A full moon this night which seemed to light up the world. A doe fed just at the edge of the shadow cast by the veranda roof while I paced, unable to sleep, along the hall and looked out into the still whiteness.

OCTOBER 21: "Beautiful but dumb" is probably an apt description of immature red-tailed hawks in the autumn. Like teenagers, they are still testing their boundaries, and their inexperience often gets them into trouble.

This afternoon, when I went out to sit on the veranda, I spotted one balanced precariously on the telephone line. As I watched it through my binoculars, it dove down into First Field and floundered around on the ground before flying up, its talons still empty, and landing on a black walnut tree near the barn. It gave me another good view and then swooped down and out of sight. In the bad old days, when all hawks were considered "varmints" and shot on sight, that bird would have been dead by now.

Instead, it soon returned to sit on a power pole above the barn overlooking my bluebird box. A pair of bluebirds fluttered closely around the hawk for several minutes as if protesting its presence, while I walked slowly toward it for a closer view. Suddenly it again dove straight at the ground, landed awkwardly on its belly, thrashed around in the dried grasses, and finally flew to a power pole behind our shed. There it perched and tore long, dangling strips from its prey—probably a rat, judging from its size—which it ate in fast gulps.

After its meal it flew to still another power pole halfway across First Field. I walked within 145 feet of its perch and lay down in the warm field grasses to watch it. Never had

I had such an opportunity to study an immature hawk close up for, as it turned out, nearly an hour. Had I been an artist, I would have had an incomparable chance to capture the colors of this particular bird. Instead, I carefully recorded its color scheme in my notebook: a brown back with white markings on its wings and reddish brown near its eyes with a light stripe over each one. Its throat and breast were white except for faint brown streaks, and it had a heavily spotted belly band, white underparts, and a black and brown horizontally striped tail with a faint white line at its edge. Glowing in the autumn sunlight, it looked far more handsome than any drawing or photograph in my field guides of the incredibly variable colors of an immature red-tailed hawk.

I spent the rest of the afternoon following it around the field from pole to pole, watching several more unsuccessful dives for prey, until it was time for me to cook our meal. But near dusk our son David reported that it was sitting in a black walnut tree beside the driveway while he watched it from his porch fifty feet away.

OCTOBER 22. The hawk was perched in a black locust tree in our front yard this morning when I opened the porch door, and the yard squirrels muttered their protests in low, grumbling undertones. Then the hawk dove into a wild rose bush after a songbird, which it missed. From there it flew to a young black walnut tree beside the driveway, and later, while I hung out the wash in the backyard, it sat on a power pole near the garage, about fifty feet away, looking alertly around. I sat down to watch it and was startled a few minutes later when it swooped within a yard of me as it headed toward the songbirds scolding in the front yard lilac bush. Once again it missed.

Two American crows appeared to taunt the hawk from the driveway. They chased it to a black walnut tree near the barn, perched above the hawk in the same tree, and cawed loudly before flying away. The hawk then flew to the power pole overlooking the bluebird box where I left it to take my morning walk. It was still in First Field, perched on still another power pole, when I returned at noon. Shortly afterward, it resumed its migration. I knew the moment it had gone because the squirrels reappeared in the yard, and the trees filled up with songbirds. But to have had so many intimate hours with an immature red-tailed hawk had lent a special aura to autumn's shining days.

OCTOBER 23. The loggers crested the mountaintop at 7:45 A.M., and Bruce was there to meet and photograph them. He talked to the logger operating the large yellow skidder for over an hour and asked permission to take pictures of their work from a safe distance, to which the man agreed. He told Bruce that they are using *two* skidders; the lumberman bought this one several weeks ago for $100,000 just to do this job. Payments on that skidder, he claimed, were $4,000 a month.

"And what will he do with it when you are finished?" Bruce asked him. The logger looked puzzled, as if such a question had never occurred to him. But he seemed proud of the machine, which was as large as a big bulldozer but on giant tires with a dozer blade in front and winches in the back for dragging several logs at the same time. He was also clearly proud of his work and proud to pose for Bruce's pictures. This man and his two colleagues are employees of our lumberman neighbor and are doing the job under the direction of his son, the same one who broke the lock and who runs the bulldozer. Bruce made it clear to the logger that while we had a legitimate quarrel with his bosses, we were concerned about the safety of the loggers.

"If there is an accident, you are welcome to use our telephone," he assured him and also told him that emergency crews have a key to the gate.

The logger seemed eager to talk and what he said gave us a little comfort. "As soon as the rains start, we will be out of here," he told Bruce. "Those slopes are too steep and dangerous when they get wet." He said that it was not economical to cut down and haul the trees at the far end of the property, and he estimated that it would take them six weeks more to thoroughly finish the job. "But, of course, it will be raining before then." He also reassured Bruce that they were not going to be cutting below the lower skid road, so Bruce did not point out that several trees had already been cut there, preferring to give him the benefit of doubt rather than arousing his anger, and hoping to save most of that 200-foot safety zone without further fighting.

Finally, the logger waxed on about all the wildlife they had seen on the property—a flock of six wild turkeys, several gray foxes, and many fox squirrels. And he agreed with Bruce that it was a beautiful day with unusually brilliant autumn color. When the talk turned to environmental subjects, he maintained that our society produces too much trash, consumes too much, and does not live lightly enough on the land. But he seemed unable to make any connections between his work and possible harm to the wildlife he admires and the environmental values he espouses. Like many people, I suppose he thinks there is plenty more where that comes from, an unending cornucopia of natural products for him to take with no thought of the morrow.

Driving up from town this morning, I felt as if I were being welcomed through the golden gates of heaven as I started up the hollow past a forest of trees turned brilliantly yellow. If only the lumberman honors his promises and stays 200 feet above the road, at least the lowest part of the hollow will be saved.

By midday it was spring-warm, and again I took an afternoon walk. The Guesthouse Trail ruffed grouse was back on his log, but scolding gray squirrels alerted him and he leaped off before I could watch him drum.

I was luckier with wild turkeys along the Far Field Road. I saw them below the road before they saw me, so I crawled to a good vantage point where I thought I would intercept them coming up Roseberry Hollow. For a while I continued to hear them scratching in the leaf duff, but then it was silent. Apparently, they had moved down, rather than uphill as I had hoped. I stretched my cramped legs, stood up, and crunched my way through the fallen leaves along the road, but still I kept a sharp lookout below. Then, halfway to the Far Field, I again spotted movement off in the understory. Slowly I sat down, this time in the middle of the road, and peered into the tangle of brush fifty feet beneath the bank.

Finally, I spotted two turkeys scratching on the forest floor and a third sitting on a heavy branch above, which I decided was the sentinel. None seemed aware of me, those dim shapes made clearer through my binoculars. After a long, quiet wait, turkeys suddenly popped up all around the three I had first spotted. Presumably, it was the end of their siesta hour. They started walking toward the road where I was sitting, but instead of climbing up the road bank, they paralleled it, trotting past in single file so that I could easily count all fifteen. Then the sentinel turkey leaped down to feed and was relieved by another, which flew up into a tree to watch. After the first fifteen turkeys disappeared, more appeared below, scratching and clucking softly. From the distance, I heard a high-pitched call, as if the fifteen were bidding farewell to the other flock.

I continued watching, sitting cross-legged on the road, and was able to count at least five foraging turkeys, but I knew there were probably more, hidden by the under-brush or resting as the others had been. At last my pa-tience was rewarded. Nineteen more turkeys, many of them with beards, filed up Roseberry Hollow, stopping to scratch as they moved along, and finally crossed the road less than thirty feet in front of me. Only then did they see me, but even so they did not panic. Instead, they milled around for a few seconds, as if deciding what to do. Then they continued on their unhurried way up the bank and out of sight.

After they disappeared, the tree sentinel flew down and it and still another hidden turkey, what I thought of as the backup sentinel, also walked up the hill, the last one cluck-ing several times to round up any possible stragglers. They too did not see me until they reached the road, but they seemed startled, as if they had fallen down on their jobs, and hastened up the bank a little faster than the main flock had. Altogether I counted thirty-six turkeys. For such shining moments I wait and watch and sometimes am rewarded.

OCTOBER 24. Overcast and humid. Could the rains be imminent? The chain saws were intermittent in the wet morning air, but the skidders hauled logs out along the ridgetop. Who really owns the mountain, I asked myself as I took my morning walk. The absentee landowners who come here rarely and only to take? Or do I, who know it in every season of the year and appreciate it for what it is, not for the money it can give me?

Later, as I settled down to rest near the Far Field Road, I heard two female downy woodpeckers calling. They flew at each other, spreading out their tail feathers, and hitched themselves up and down the same tree trunks, all the while emitting their ratchety calls. A nearby foraging male downy ignored them, but both a white-breasted nuthatch and a tufted titmouse scolded. The downies pursued each other, opening and closing their wings, with their heads and bills pointed upward. They continued this interplay for at least ten minutes until they finally flew off. That, according to the experts, was the bill-waving display, supposedly given only in the winter and early spring prior to breeding. How little we know about the private lives of even the commonest birds.

A gentle rain started and I sat under my umbrella, listening to the keening of cedar waxwings and the steady sifting down of leaves. Six weeks of rain, I prayed, and maybe the wilderness grove would be saved, at least for another winter. The rain picked up momentum and I cheered inwardly—Come on Rain! But it petered out once I returned home, and I heard the laboring skidders off and on most of the day.

OCTOBER 25. More signs of the incipient rutting season. Along the Far Field Road I found a primary scrape. The area had been newly scratched up and a pile of fresh deer scat deposited a foot from it. A broken branch hung down which the buck had probably hooked with his antlers, pulling it low enough so he could reach it easily. Then he probably chewed on it, covering it with his saliva, and rubbed it with his forehead scent glands. After rubbing, he would have pawed the ground beneath the branch, opening it up and creating, in this case, a shallow, saucer-like depression in the earth two feet in diameter.

Next, he must have stood in the center of the scrape and, according to Leonard Lee Rue III, a naturalist who has observed and photographed bucks making primary scrapes, the buck would have balanced himself on his two front feet, rubbed the hock or tarsal glands of his hind feet together, and urinated on them. In that way, the urine and the tarsal scent washed down on to the scrape beneath, giving it a muddy appearance. He also defecated. Such scrapes are usually made by dominant bucks along major deer trails, but lesser bucks may also cautiously visit them. The bucks return again and again to the scrapes, renewing their scent each time. These scrapes are basically advertising posts, indicating to does that the bucks are present and available for breeding.

OCTOBER 26. Warming, with a heavy, rose-colored fog at dawn. The fog did not start to lift until after ten this morning. I slipped quietly up the Guesthouse Trail and surprised the ruffed grouse standing on his moldering log. He remained still for several minutes before slowly descending, like a king from his throne, and walking majestically off into the woods. I retreated back down the trail and waited for him to return and start drumming. After a few minutes, I heard a partial drumroll as he started up again. I crept near and saw him on the log, but he saw me too and slipped off, this time for good. For a couple of years now, I have played this same game with this grouse, but so far he has won every time.

People often suggest that I should set up a blind near the drumming log, but I prefer to watch without a blind, becoming a part of the scene instead of a mere spectator. Peering from a blind may be necessary to capture the best wildlife photographs, but not to capture wildlife in print. In fact, once the animals forget I am sitting there, I can often scribble notes as they go about their affairs.

Ruffed grouse, though, lose their caution only in spring. Then they wander heedlessly up and down our hollow road in lovesick fogs while I sit and watch. But in the autumn they are warier, especially since the fall drumming I've been watching is being performed by an older, resident ruffed grouse as a way of telling the newly dispersed young ones that the territory is already occupied. Later, drumming will be done by newly established young males and will steadily increase throughout November so that their claim to a new territory is strengthened. But I have discovered that here on our mountaintop grouse drumming can occur any month of the year, even on a warm day in mid-winter.

OCTOBER 27. Another weekend, and time for Bruce to take his "after" photos. They are leaving nothing. Every side hollow leading down to the road was cut clean, and they have reached and almost finished cutting the wilderness grove. I was like a child in a horror story, drawn to see what has happened, yet not able to fully believe the depths of the destruction.

The section beyond Margaret's derelict house, the area where they first started, was treeless except for a few hopelessly crippled young trees. The soil was powdery dust, devoid of any greenery, even weeds, and huge piles of slash lay everywhere. This logging is by far the worst job anyone has done here since the mountain was clear-cut in the early nineteenth century. It looked as if the land was being cleared for house lots.

I sat beneath what was left of the wilderness grove at the end of what was once the Upper Road. Leaves sifted down around me, the last leaves these trees will ever contribute to the forest soil because unless it starts raining within the next couple of days the trees are doomed. Huge piles of cut trees lay along the top of the ridge trail— stacked bodies waiting to be hauled away. And they had started clearing the mountaintop too. I am finally convinced that they really are clear-cutting the entire property, not selectively timbering as they had so often promised they would do. What other promises will they break? Will they stay 200 feet above the hollow road?

I cried most of the way back home, mourning the death

of the innocents as I scuffed through the dust, sweating in the sun. A verdant mountainside made desert in a couple of weeks. How will the biosphere escape the ravaging greed of humanity and its machines?

OCTOBER 28. On this windy, cold day a raptor-bander set up his lure pole and bow net in the middle of First Field. The winds were north-northwest, and red-tails were "slope-soaring" on the wind. He baited his lure pole with a large homing pigeon which he protected with a leather jacket already covered with talon marks. Using such jackets cuts down on pigeon mortality, he told me. He also explained "trapper's rush"—the excitement he feels as he watches a hawk dive at the trap. All the while he set up, red-tails kept flying over high in the sky.

Finally, dressed in camouflage, I crouched behind his wooden blind, while he stood behind the blind scanning for hawks. As soon as he saw one, he too crouched down, watching carefully through a slit, and then twitched the line to which the pigeon was attached to make it flap enticingly. But not one hawk even stopped to look.

"There are days when you see a million hawks, and not one of them will come down. It's like they've eaten, and now they want to go wherever it is they're going," he told me. "Hawk migration trapping is all a matter of geography, position, and weather."

Since his position, above the powerline right-of-way on First Field, was not working, I climbed to the top of First Field to check the action. Four red-tails and one sharp-shinned hawk flew up over the ridge and hovered above the field, so I started down to tell him. But he had already crested the ridge, and as we stood discussing the possibility of changing the trap site, a mature bald eagle hove into sight. It not only flew over, but it flew in *low*, circling several times above our heads like a good luck omen. Even without binoculars we could clearly see its white head and tail shining in the sunlight—the best and closest view I've ever had of a bald eagle here. Was it just because I was spending much of the day intently studying the sky?

After we relocated, there was the usual midday lull. The few red-tails we saw stayed high, their heads pointed toward town instead of toward the trap. We simply could not get their attention. Soaring, not eating, was definitely their priority on such a cold, windswept day. And as the day progressed, they soared higher and higher until they were mere specks in a field of limitless blue.

I never had a chance to experience "trapper's rush," but I did spend an exhilarating day on the ridge, watching the spectacular view and admiring the vivid autumn colors and clouds of varying shapes floating serenely past. When we finally packed it in for the day and added up our totals we had seen three sharp-shinned hawks, two Cooper's hawks, innumerable turkey vultures, fifty-eight red-tailed hawks, and, best of all, our special bald eagle sighting which compensated for our unsuccessful attempt at banding.

OCTOBER 29. The continual dry, beautiful weather mocks me. Always before I have rejoiced in such glorious weather; now my enjoyment is bittersweet as the trees keep toppling. But even if it would start raining tomorrow, it is too late for the wilderness grove. I have not slept well for many days and about all I have energy for is to lurch around our woods, write notes, write letters, and brood. I will die someday in autumn and dead leaves will sift down and cover my grave as they now fall on me alive, sitting beneath an enormous red oak tree on our property.

The flaming trees of autumn are a reminder of earth's end, the fire next time, fire, not ice as poet Robert Frost speculated. Is it not raining now because we have already irreversibly set the earth on destruct, having polluted and heated it beyond its capacity to recover? I am afraid we will not recognize the point of no return until we have passed it. To most people, if the landscape looks pretty, then it is all right. If there are more turkeys and deer than ever, nothing is wrong.

Walking through the dried goldenrod at the Far Field, I stirred up dozens of dark-eyed juncos that had been nestled on the ground, silently eating and soaking in the golden sunlight of this perfect day. In late afternoon the yard filled up with eastern bluebirds. They landed on the wires near the barn, shifting positions and fluttering down into the weeds. Near dusk the deer filed down from the field and across the lawn. We still have our peaceable kingdom here, at least after the loggers leave each day and before buck season begins.

Tonight, as we were driving up the hollow after an Audubon meeting, a saw-whet owl flew in front of us and then landed on a low, overhanging tree branch beside the road. Bruce screeched to a halt. Excitedly we peered out the window at the small, motionless creature that perched less than twenty feet away. We had never seen a saw-whet before and could not believe our luck. Its yellow eyes gleamed in the dark as it returned our gaze. Finally, after five minutes of mutual contemplation, the owl flew off into the woods.

Ever since I had first seen a picture of this smallest owl in eastern North America, I had wanted to find one in the woods. Yet my chances for that seemed slim. Saw-whet owls (*Aegolius acadicus*), formerly called Acadian owls, prefer northern evergreen forests or swamps for their nesting grounds. They do most of their hunting of white-footed mice, their favorite prey, at night and are shy, retiring creatures. But they do like to occupy old northern flicker holes, which we have in abundance. They also have been known to poke their heads out of holes during the day if the trees are rapped sharply. However, I had been knocking on such trees ever since we moved to the mountain, and neither saw-whet owls nor any other creatures had responded to my summons.

Saw-whet owls are small creatures, only seven and a half to eight and a half inches long with a wingspread of eighteen inches. They live as far west as southeastern Alaska and California and as far east as Nova Scotia and New Brunswick. Researchers have recorded them as breeding birds in north-central Pennsylvania, but they rarely nest in the southern states.

Saw-whets are named for the noise they make during their breeding season between March and May, a sound resembling the filing of a saw blade. In addition, they have a wide variety of other calls they make more frequently: a robinlike whistle, a "whurdle-whurdle" call, and a "tang-tang" that resembles an anvil. As owls go, though, saw-whets are unusually quiet most of the time.

After a short courtship they find an abandoned northern flicker hole and lay four to seven white, almost round eggs on top of wood chips left by the woodpeckers. The female lays an egg every two to three days and begins brooding after the first or second egg is laid, so the owlets hatch at widely spaced intervals. Researchers who have found saw-whet nests claim there is almost total survival of the young—an unusual occurrence in the owl world.

For many years ornithologists were not certain whether some saw-whet owls migrate. Yet their bodies were often found among those of migrating songbirds that had been killed during severe weather. Two ornithologists, Geoffrey L. Holroyd and John G. Woods, conducted a fifteen-year study from 1955 until 1969 of migrating saw-whet owls in eastern North America. During those years they banded 4,802 owls and discovered two major eastern migration routes. One begins in central Ontario and moves southwest through the Ohio River Valley into Kentucky, and the other follows the Atlantic coastal lowlands from Maine to Georgia. Their spring migration extends from March first until the end of May and their fall migration from September first through November thirtieth.

Obviously, central Pennsylvania does not lie in either of the main migration routes. However, a saw-whet owl that was banded in north-central Pennsylvania by Holroyd and Woods was later recovered in Georgia, so there is some migration through our area. The owl we saw tonight was, in all likelihood, a late migrant. But I was amused by the serendipity that allowed us to see our first saw-whet owl on the way home from an Audubon meeting.

OCTOBER 30. Two years ago today the weather was also warm and beautiful, and the continuous Indian summer weather had played into the hands of the lumberman who had begun building his logging roads. Then, as now, I felt compelled to watch the destruction from the hollow road. I could hear the bulldozer long before I reached the first pulloff. The hollow reverberated with the screeching of the machine and the crashing of trees. It sounded as if a demonic force had been let loose. I could smell the odor of raw dirt and broken trees as I sat below on the road watching the destruction. The bulldozer operator, the lumberman's son, kept backing up, then pushing the machine forward, toppling everything in its path. The machine rattled and clanked with the effort, and a large rock tumbled several hundred feet down the slope and into the road beside me as I watched.

When the bulldozer halted, the forester came down the road, full of friendly smiles and camaraderie. He, after all, directed the operation and had found the gap in the property line that allowed the lumberman to "harvest" his land.

"How are you?" he asked pleasantly, and I honestly replied, "Not so good as I watch the bulldozer." So he spent over an hour justifying what they were doing, claiming that they would do such an excellent job of cutting that we would be pleased by the results and would never notice the loss of the few trees they planned to take.

"The hollow will look the same," he promised. Most large trees such as the tulip poplars and the white pines would be left as seed trees. "My boss will protest some of the big ones I will insist on leaving, but he will let me make the decisions," the forester assured me. "That's the difference between my boss and most other lumbermen. He is one of the few who hires a forester and then listens to him."

He did admit that he planned to clear-cut some of the flat areas farther up the mountainside, but he claimed that the roads they were building would be properly contoured and reseeded after the cutting. He seemed to be sincere, convinced that his boss was honest and wanted only to do what was best for the land. However, he could not resist praising the merits of the red oak trees.

"The red oak in Blair County is the best in the world," he said, and that was the species they were chiefly interested in.

The lumberman himself, he told me, was busy building the road on our neighbor's property, "pushing" it, as he put it. All the while we talked, the son continued "pushing" his own bulldozer, crossing the last ravine before the big pulloff and then, as the lumberman commented, "met his match" as he continually charged ahead and then pulled back, boulders crashing down and often resisting the powerful machine.

The forester seemed compelled to justify what they were doing and what they planned to do, even then. But after an hour of trying to be pleasant, I attempted to excuse myself. Like the ancient mariner, he held me in thrall, using the force of his convictions instead of his eyes. Over and over he repeated what a wonderful man his boss was and how little he was interested in money.

"What is truth?" I asked myself as I walked back up the road. And I continue to ask myself that about this whole sad episode every day.

This afternoon I scattered dark-eyed juncos when I stepped outside. The sun poured down unfettered by leaves, and I crunched loudly through a layer of dry leaves as I walked. A dandelion blossomed in the driveway; the myrtle was out in front of the guesthouse. But along Laurel Ridge Trail I stopped short in utter shock: four wild azalea shrubs were in bloom, the dried, dead, spring blossoms still dangling below the new blossoms. It seemed unnatural, something I had never observed before—a portent of imminent disaster.

OCTOBER 31. It was raining hard when I pulled on Bruce's rubbers over my moccasins and grabbed the old black umbrella held together by four paper clips and several loops of thread. Because of the weather, I dressed appropriately—baggy wool slacks, torn blue jacket, and several layers of shirts and sweaters to keep out the dampness.

When I stepped outside I was instantly overwhelmed by birdsong. Hundreds of robins sang and called from the treetops, and for a minute I thought it was early spring rather than mid-autumn. Like Ulysses, I was drawn irresistibly by those siren calls and others of a dozen bird species. It was as if all the birds heading south had landed on the mountain to wait out the first substantial rain in months.

Ruby-crowned kinglets and white-throated sparrows ate the dried grapes hanging from the top of the old apple tree. A flock of northern flickers flew up from the driveway. Dark-eyed juncos bent the dried field weeds down as they plucked out the seeds. Gray squirrels were also abroad, running up and down tree trunks with black walnuts in their mouths.

The frenzied noise and activity of birds and squirrels pulled me up past the old garden, across the powerline right-of-way and into the woods where more robins called. Even after I left the bird zone and began a silent, sodden trek up the trail, the pungent smell of newly fallen, wet leaves was enough to keep me walking. Despite the gathering mist, the woods glowed with the yellow of fallen leaves and the less brassy yellow of witch hazel blossoms in the understory. The soft color of this latest of flowering trees resembles the muted shades of early spring blossoms rather than the bold, bright autumnal hues.

A flock of cedar waxwings wheeled overhead; a ruffed grouse exploded from the underbrush. I could hear calls form a flock of American goldfinches. But I had walked a couple miles and the rain had begun to soak over my rubber tops and penetrate the thin defenses of the old umbrella. I started anticipating a hot cup of coffee.

The birds were still calling as I neared the house, and I was momentarily stopped by the sound and movement all around me. There was no doubt, though, that the frenzy was dying down. But I was grateful to have experienced a special autumn spectacle of life and color which is possible only during a rainy, late October morning.

November

Ages must have passed before man gained sufficient mental stature to pay admiring tribute to the tree standing in all the glory of its full leafage, shimmering in the sunlight, making its myriad bows to the restless winds; but eons must have lapsed before the human eye grew keen enough and the human soul large enough to give sympathetic comprehension to the beauty of bare branches laced across changing skies; which is the treelover's full heritage.

—Anna Comstock, *Trees at Leisure*

NOVEMBER 1. A beautiful, warm, clear, Indian summer day with a breeze that floated the milkweed seed across the field in silken puffs. The ruffed grouse was drumming on his log by eight this morning, counterpoint to the loggers already hard at work. I met an old friend in the post office the other day, and when she asked, "How are you?" I replied, "They are clear-cutting the mountainside above our road." She acted as if she had not heard me, as if being concerned with such an issue simply was not important. She and her husband are thoroughly caught up in the humanitarian issues of the area. To be worried about a few trees probably struck her as ludicrous.

Trees have no standing, especially on private land. The unspoken opinion, whenever I answer someone honestly about how I am, is that it's none of my business what a property owner is doing on his or her land. We used to say that about child and wife abuse too—none of our business, a family affair. Those ideas have changed now, and we are expected to report human abusive situations to the proper authorities. Dare I hope that ideas about how a person treats the land will also change soon?

Another friend, seeking to comfort me said, "In a few years, it will be filled with wildlife." That's like saying to someone who has lost a child, "You can always have more." Of course, but not that particular child, not that particular woods. Bruce says it is more like telling a husband after his wife has been raped, "She'll recover."

I sat below the Far Field Road and listened to American robins, cedar waxwings, blue jays, Carolina wrens, eastern bluebirds, northern cardinals, a pileated woodpecker, white-throated sparrows, dark-eyed juncos, and American goldfinches calling. A couple of Carolina wrens landed with a "thud" behind me on the tree I was sitting against, scolded loudly, and then flew on as if annoyed that I had usurped a favorite tree. All the while a gray squirrel on a limb above my head threw bark and twigs down as it foraged. I had, for a short time, been absorbed into the scene around me, and the wild creatures went about their business as if I were not there.

Later, I found a cozy bed of freshly fallen leaves to lie down in and watch a flock of European starlings wheel in and out, harvesting wild grapes overhead. But they were quickly routed by the dozens and dozens of cedar waxwings that dominated the hanging vines. Once, though, an eastern bluebird landed, called, and snatched a few grapes before flying off. Wherever I lay or sat or walked today, the witch hazel cast a golden haze on the woods, its fruity smell mingling with the odor of fallen leaves—elixir of autumn.

At the Far Field, a hermit thrush flew up from the ground above the old fox den, perched on a branch, and chipped and dipped its rufous-colored tail up and down as I watched. Then a dragonfly landed on a goldenrod stem, and I noted both blue and green marks on its black body. It was a creature of delicate Oriental beauty, its translucent wings shimmering in the brilliant autumnal light.

Above the Far Field thicket, I looked up the hill to see a doe running hard toward me. Suddenly she veered off just as a buck came over the hill snorting like a bull. Turning, she fled back up the hill, the buck in hot pursuit.

Coming back down the First Field Trail, I flushed an American woodcock from an intermittent wet area. Judging from the probe holes in the mud, the bird had stopped off during migration to hunt for earthworms, its preferred food.

I ended this glorious first day of November by sitting out on the veranda basking in the sunlight. At 3:45 an eastern phoebe flew in, landed on the lilac bush, and flicked its tail. That is the latest date ever recorded for a phoebe here. Next a male northern flicker called from the top of a black walnut tree. Even the katydids tuned up, weakly, slowly, and in diminished numbers, but definitely still alive. Almost as if it wanted to make certain that I identified it properly, the phoebe returned twice, landing each time in a tree beside the veranda. The first time it caught an insect as I watched; the second time it "chipped," flipped its tail, and allowed me a minute to study it thoroughly through my binoculars.

Near dusk, four deer fed on the lawn and in the barn-yard. Then there were five deer, and all crossed the stream and headed up the slope toward me. From somewhere a sixth one materialized, and for a moment I felt as if I might be mobbed. The deer looked up and sniffed in my direction, and when I turned a page in my book, one deer snorted. All evaporated in an instant, almost as if they had been mirages, wavering on the edge of my consciousness. Amazing how quickly wild animals can disappear and reappear, almost like the Cheshire cat's grin in *Alice in Wonderland*.

Then I heard the faint strains of a great horned owl calling from Sapsucker Ridge. Finally, the phoebe flew into the lilac bush for the evening, just as a jet plane plummeted downward—resembling a rosy, slow-moving comet as it caught the last light of day.

NOVEMBER 2. Another Indian summer day. Birds were abroad everywhere I walked. Blackbird noise lured me from Laurel Ridge Trail off through the woods and over to the edge of the mountain, where I found hundreds of European starlings interspersing their usual low-pitched blackbird chatter with high-pitched screams. I sat quietly on the ground and watched as a small flock wheeled in, silencing the larger flock. Then they all took off, flying in unison, circling once, and returning to land in the same trees and continue the same chattering and screaming. All wore the speckled black and white coats and brown wings of starling winter plumage. Occasionally I discerned songs reminiscent of eastern meadowlarks, but I never saw any, so what I heard were starling imitations.

Cedar waxwings also swirled about in flocks. Both species were attracted by the black birch tree cones filled with seeds. Small flocks of starlings flew in closer to me to land in the birch branches, fluttering and pecking at the cones like overgrown kinglets in what seemed to be periodical feeding frenzies. Many birds remained sitting quietly in sentinel trees along the mountaintop, but others broke off into smaller flocks to move up and down the trees or onto others, always in unison as if there could be no individualists. The longer I sat, the closer they came. Even though they were the common, despised European starlings, I found them fascinating, a faint reminder of what it must have been like here years ago when many native bird species, such as the passenger pigeons, formed immense flocks that darkened the skies.

Finally, I resumed my walk, rejoicing in the baring bones of late autumn. Although the woods were noisy, crackling with all the newly fallen leaves, the landscape had opened up, making it easy for me to observe not only the European starlings, but the calling hairy woodpecker and mouse-colored brown creeper as they foraged on tree trunks. I paused once to watch a pair of song sparrows sitting in a locust sapling and ruffling their feathers in the warming rays of sun. I suspected they were father and son since the one sang brilliantly while the other had that disconsolate look of inexperienced youth.

Not all the wildflowers were dead yet. I found two small stalks of Queen Anne's lace newly blooming among older, dried seed heads. These I gathered, along with the dried spikes of moth mullein and common mullein, some opened milkweed pods, and the polished, mahogany-colored fertile spikes of sensitive ferns for the beginnings of a winter bouquet.

Eventually I wended my way homeward and again spent the late afternoon on the veranda, gathering up memories and warmth for the coming winter. A red-tailed hawk circled in the quickening wind of afternoon, casting its dark shadow on the lawn and dazzling me with the white of its breast and the red brown of its tail. At dusk I walked again, startling two deer in the weeds down near the barn, and watched a flight of ducks high overhead. Every tree and bush, every grass blade and weed head, was lit with the deepening scarlet and purple of another fantastic Pinatubo sunset; that faraway volcanic eruption in the Philippines months ago still affects our sunsets evening after evening. As darkness finally descended over woods and fields, peace settled like a mantle on the land, and I gave thanks for one more day of Indian summer.

NOVEMBER 3. Cold, windy, and not much warming as this weekend day progressed. But it was clear and beautiful, so I headed down the hollow.

Four deer grazed around Margaret's yard and down to the almost dry stream, but they did not startle or even pay attention as I walked past. Later, a buck halfway up the Laurel Ridge side did startle and crash on out of sight. I identified a couple of winter wrens, a pair of downy woodpeckers, one ruffed grouse, black-capped chickadees, dark-eyed juncos, a white-breasted nuthatch, a brown creeper, and golden-crowned kinglets along the road, although I saw more of them walking back when the sun finally began to penetrate the depths of the hollow.

At last I squared my shoulders and started up the last side hollow on the lumberman's land. Still, I hesitated to once again face the destruction. I sat for a while, looking down the side hollow and across at pristine Laurel Ridge. Sitting there it was possible to imagine a wilderness woods, especially since the Sunday silence had muted the usual intrusive technological sounds from the valley. The hunters too must desist for this one day of peace a week. But ahead of me, I knew, lay desecration.

Again I procrastinated and followed the Lower Road out to the end where no cutting had yet been done. I stopped to lie against the road bank, gazing down and across at uncut woods, deluding myself that nothing had changed. Finally, I forced myself up and back into the cutting zone.

The wilderness grove was gone—totally trashed—and the yellow bulldozer was posed on the top knoll, triumphant in what it had accomplished with the help of puny men. A few small trees were left. Several large stumps were hollow, but the trees had been cut down anyway. Other stumps were solid, three and a half feet wide at the base. Where once there had been a verdant forest, covered with layers of leaves and soil, now only the bare, scraped bones of the knoll were left, baking in the sun. I couldn't even tell where the Upper Road had been because of the churned-up soil and slash in every direction.

As Thoreau once wrote so tellingly in *Walden,* "How can you expect the birds to sing when their groves are cut down?" How indeed? The forest of singing, calling birds was gone, leaving only silence. Not the silence of Sunday's balm, but the silence of death and finality. Never in my lifetime would there be another wilderness grove here.

NOVEMBER 4. A cold, seventeen degrees at dawn, barely climbing to a chilly, breezy, intermittently sunshiny twenty-five degrees by midday. Time to hang the bird feeders from the back porch. The regulars have been coming in for several days—white-breasted nuthatches, tufted titmice, black-capped chickadees—and calling as if to remind me that the feeders are still not out. We have an old, battered wooden feeder that long ago lost its sides and has been repaired several times, but, being sentimentalists, we hate to replace it. This, after all, was our first bird feeder, bought when we lived in Maine twenty-five years ago and packed with our other valuables when we moved here in August 1971 with our three small sons.

The other feeder is a gift from an Audubon friend who specializes in designing unique feeders out of throwaways, in this case two large plastic soda containers reincarnated as an impregnable tube feeder. To complete our low-cost setup, we scatter seed on the back steps below the feeder and on the ground beneath the steps. Since we are surrounded by wild food—staghorn sumac, old grape vines,

pokeberries, and weed seeds of every conceivable species—we don't bother with too many artificial feeders.
And I rarely put out suet either since our woodpeckers
have a whole mountain of trees from which to glean insect
food. Even when I have put it out, it gets very little attention. What I have discovered over my years of bird
feeding is that our feeder species prefer either black oil
sunflower seed or white millet and so that is what I buy,
three hundred pounds, more or less, depending on the se-
verity of the late autumn and winter. Usually we feed the
birds until late April, again depending on how late spring
is. Often more seeds are eaten in March and April than in
mid-winter, since by then many of the wild food sources
have been consumed.

It takes only a few hours after the feeders have been
scrubbed and hung for the first birds to notice them and
spread the word. Today a Carolina wren, black-capped
chickadees, tufted titmice, and white-breasted nuthatches
discovered the bird feeders at the same time and appeared
to be calling in their friends.

White-tailed deer romances continued apace, and as we
sat eating breakfast at 6:45 in the early morning light we
watched a two-point buck in the yard sniffing the wind
for a doe in estrus. Apparently he had no luck, so he
bounded back into the weeds of First Field. Researchers
claim that cold weather and decreasing amounts of light
stimulate the onset of the breeding season; dark, rainy autumns encourage earlier breeding, probably because the
deer's eyes are getting less light. On the other hand, both
obesity and a poor diet on the part of the doe may delay
breeding. But, depending on the quality of the range, a
white-tailed doe fawn may breed the year she is born.
Most bucks seem to wait until they are a year and a half
old, but research on that is still scanty. Regardless of when
they breed, a doe is only receptive for twenty-four hours,

but the buck is in rut for sixty days, breeding with anywhere from four to twenty does over that period.

I have been reading Richard K. Nelson's *The Island Within*. Although it is set in Alaska, what he has to say about a sense of place rings a responsive bell inside of me. "As time went by," he writes, "I also realized that the particular place I'd chosen was less important than the fact that I'd chosen a place and focused my life around it. . . . What makes a place special is the way it buries itself inside the heart. . . . My hope is to acclaim the rewards of exploring the place in which a person lives rather than searching afar, of becoming fully involved with the near-at-hand, and of nurturing a deeper relationship with home" (p. xii).

I feel the same way about our mountaintop and hollow. If only Americans would learn that there is a whole universe of interest in their own backyards, despite the allure of travel to more exotic places, more picture-postcard beautiful places. So much nature writing today, both in books and magazines, celebrates the faraway. For instance, there are more books and studies about Africa's big mammals than there are of any of the smaller mammals here. Finding detailed information on the life histories of porcupines, red and gray foxes, even the various squirrel species to verify my own observations, can be difficult. Only recently have books been written on a few of those animals, but much more needs to be done. Backyard naturalists, instead of just backyard birders (who are far more common), should be encouraged to watch and learn. Until a majority of people learn to appreciate the natural world through their own observations, I fear that we will continue to destroy it.

Back in 1964 the English ornithologist James Fisher and our own Roger Tory Peterson co-authored a book called *The World of Birds*. In it they declared that "the cult of the

useless is coming to power—useless flowers, useless butterflies, useless warblers and singing birds, useless hawks,
useless fossils, useless wilderness: all the useless things
that by their very uselessness are useful . . . redeeming and
refreshing and needful to the human spirit" (p. 261). That
cult, however, seems to still be limited to a minority of
people, otherwise, why would the skidders continue
screaming over the mountainside, slashing everything in
their way? The lumberman regards wildflowers, butterflies, nongame mammals, and birds as truly useless, and
the forest remains useless if it is unharvested.

NOVEMBER 5. Depths of January weather in early November—fourteen degrees at dawn and clear. But the
drummer was on his log shortly after nine this morning
and finally flew off when I approached him. Along Laurel
Ridge Trail, when I paused I heard another grouse drumming. It is impossible to move quietly in the woods with
the crackling leaves on the ground, so I must stop in order
to hear anything.

While I was taking off my boots on the back porch, a
chipmunk came up the steps to eat dropped bird seed. It
paused on the bottom step in a begging position, paws up
as if in supplication when it saw me, but when I didn't
move it ignored me. I watched as it systematically cleaned
off each step and then reached the porch itself, siphoning
up seeds between the garbage cans and puffing its cheeks
full of booty. Finally, it crossed the porch, ran across my
boots and up my jean-clad leg to my knee. Then it scampered back down again. It investigated my other foot and
eventually went off into the weeds while I sat reliving the
feeling of a chipmunk climbing up my leg. Hoping to
bring it back, I drove it off instead by scattering more seed
on the steps. It ran into the grape tangle beneath the back
porch where it climbed up the weed stalks to harvest wild

seeds. As I continued sitting there a dark-eyed junco, black-capped chickadees, and white-breasted nuthatches went about the business of snatching seeds from the feeder and flying off to crack and eat them.

NOVEMBER 6. American goldfinches, house finches, and northern cardinals discovered the bird feeders this morning, along with increasing numbers of tufted titmice, black-capped chickadees, dark-eyed juncos, white-breasted nuthatches, and the Carolina wren. Eastern bluebirds also called in the yard this morning, and in the strengthening, warming sun of early afternoon, I found singing American robins at the Far Field.

Ten golden-crowned kinglets gathered around me when I "pished," a couple dancing less than six feet from where I stood. Incessantly piping their high-pitched "zeezees," they were behind me, beside me, above me, below me. For a few moments I felt like the pied piper of kinglets. But they were quickly off in a whirl of "zees," moving restlessly through the woods at fluttering speed.

Once they were out of earshot, a flock of eastern bluebirds called overhead. Eastern bluebirds and golden-crowned kinglets—twelve years ago seeing either was an unexpected pleasure. Now both are abundant along with that other newcomer breeder, the red-bellied woodpecker. No matter how regularly the seasons seem to unfold, nature is never static.

I walked into the Far Field thicket to watch the annual drunken antics of American robins and cedar waxwings as they fed on the fermented berries of the Hercules' clubs. The cedar waxwings' breasts glowed golden in the sunshine, while their yellow tail bands reflected the light. The American robins sang as they fed, but the cedar waxwings just perched and gorged. I sat down nearby, eager to observe the color and action of one of autumn's best shows here. Although I did see a northern flicker eating and heard an eastern bluebird call, it was primarily a robin and waxwing sound and light show—their last orgy before winter sets in.

Do the oldtimers look forward to this drunken binge in late autumn? Is there a time when the alcoholic content of the berries is just perfect? The waxwings managed to retain their staid, unruffled, slick, businesslike demeanor, but the robins resembled bumbling, restless, overgrown schoolboys on their first bar crawl. Both species fluttered like butterflies as they tried to balance themselves on the tops of the bent-over berry heads to eat. The robins also scratched in the leaves and poked in the earth. Perhaps they don't believe in drinking on an empty stomach.

In the woods beyond the Far Field more cedar waxwings were harvesting, but this time it was wild grapes draped high in the trees. Against the deep blue sky dozens of cedar waxwings coursed back and forth above me, and grapes pattered down like raindrops. A couple of European starlings uttering low-pitched growls also joined in the feast of the grapes. The longer I sat, the more grapes I saw and the more birds flew in. One tree held at least a dozen waxwings, another several robins, and I could hear an entire flock of starlings somewhere nearby, but the three species did not intermingle.

Suddenly, seventy waxwings took off in synchronized flight. I looked up to see a red-tailed hawk floating silently below treetop level. Most of the waxwings did not return, but the starlings remained even though the hawk made a second pass overhead, spiraling higher in the sky. Once the hawk was gone for good, though, the waxwings returned and then the starlings took off.

Finally I walked to the second thicket and found the Hercules' club berry heads crowded with dozens of waxwings. Everywhere I looked there were waxwings, probably hundreds altogether. Flocking birds seem to be controlled by a single mind because they would fly together from berry clump to berry clump, ignoring other clumps just as crowded with berries.

During this wonderful day in the thickets among the Hercules' club, I was reminded of the time I first discovered those shrubby trees during an early snow in October. I heard American robins singing and found them and cedar waxwings eating the berries. So intent were they that I was able to sit directly below the ten-foot-high tree they were feeding on, my head less than six feet away from the flock. Later, I learned that the Hercules' club (*Aralia spinosa*) has one of the largest compound leaves of any tree, often three feet in length and from two to two and a half feet in width with numerous short-stalked leaflets, each of which are from two to three inches long. In fact, I swear they thud when they hit the ground in early autumn.

In the winter their clublike twigs are particularly noticeable, accounting for their common name, and so are their incredibly stout thorns and prickles, hence *spinosa*. Despite this protective armor, though, white-tailed deer browse heavily on their trunks and stems during the winter, often girdling them as completely as a porcupine would. For a long time I thought that the damage I was seeing was caused by porcupines even though nothing I read indicated that they ate this tree. But finding a maze of deer tracks in the snow throughout a grove of Hercules' clubs proved they were the culprits.

They bloom here in August, huge masses of white blossoms buzzing with bees and other insects. Known also as the "angelica-tree" and "devil's club," they usually grow no more than ten to twenty feet in height, although occasionally trees have been found nearly forty feet tall with trunks as thick as twelve inches. Ranging from southern New York to Missouri and south to Florida and Texas, they grow best in well-drained, fertile soils, but often occur on dry and stony slopes, the situation here. Furthermore, they grow only in south-facing thickets on the mountaintop.

Their abundant umbels of ovoid, black berries provide food for many species of wild birds, but I notice that they are usually eaten only after most of the wild grapes, pokeberries, and wild black cherries are gone. But once they start, the birds will strip every berry in only a few days.

NOVEMBER 7. Once again I began my sun-worshiping days just as most human sun worshipers have quit for the season. Like the wild animals, I seek shade in the summer and sunny, sheltered nooks in the late autumn and winter. The sun and light mean more to me when there is less of it. So I lay back against the bank of the Far Field Road this morning, basking in the warmth. All I heard were cedar waxwings and a faint train whistle, a northern flicker and a red-bellied woodpecker. When I finally stood up, a doe stared unbelievingly at me from twenty feet away down the bank and then leaped off. Two male northern cardinals chased each other. A pileated woodpecker called and then, over and over, I heard a rufous-sided towhee! I found him in a tangle of fallen tree branches beside the Far Field Road, a lovely male, "towheeing" for all he was worth, and, incidentally, setting another late bird record, this time for towhees, on the mountain.

At the Far Field in a clump of four black locust trees I discovered one with its bark freshly shredded from the ground to at least fifteen feet high. Much of the inner bark still hung in strips from the tree, but there were also piles of it on the ground. Probably it was the work of a small black bear, since the tree was not big enough to support the weight of a large one. They often mark their territory in such a way, or, in this case, maybe they were just practicing.

I came back along the Short Circuit Trail and stopped

again to rest. I heard a rustle in the woods and an eight-point buck ran up and stopped twenty feet away from where I was sitting on a fallen log. He never saw me. First he stopped to rub his rack on a laurel bush, then he walked majestically on, right across the trail, turned, looked straight toward me and proceeded slowly onward. I never moved, which is why he never did realize I was there; the wind, for once, was in my favor. On the other hand there is no denying the fact that at this time of year bucks have only one thing on their minds—sex!

NOVEMBER 8. A sodden world with a dim sun in a white sky. Fingers of fog drifted across the valley below, but I could see strips of green and brown earth through the vapor. Blue jays shrieked in the mostly silent world, although sharp ears could distinguish the calls of tufted titmice, eastern bluebirds, white-breasted nuthatches, black-capped chickadees, American goldfinches, and golden-crowned kinglets. Of course, absolute silence doesn't exist here. A day like this draws the valley noises like a magnet, train whistles and machines screaming from the limestone quarry being the most intrusive, with the exception of the continual logging next door. Gunshots, too, frequently shatter the peace.

Several dozen American goldfinches, calling as they worked, plucked winged nutlets from the cones of the black birch trees near the old dump area. I also spotted two pine siskins mingling with the goldfinches, scolding and chasing each other. Dozens of additional goldfinches fed on the dried goldenrod seeds, the weed heads bowing under their weight. Suddenly they flew up and out of the weeds, directly overhead—a storm of goldfinches, many pausing on branches directly above me. When I finally walked on, I discovered twenty-four American gold-finches, two pine siskins, and two dark-eyed juncos feeding on the cones of a small black birch tree at the edge of the powerline right-of-way. They were joined by a golden-crowned kinglet. All the birds swung from the limbs like high-wire, trapeze artists, scolding each other as they foraged.

The American goldfinch (*Carduelis tristis*) is one of the most widely distributed of the North American songbirds, breeding from coast to coast and from southern Canada throughout most of the United States. In winter they can be found wherever there is plentiful food in the form of weed and tree seeds or heavily stocked bird feeders. According to Cornell University's Feeder Watch statistics, American goldfinches are one of the most common species to visit bird feeders nationwide, preferring to eat sunflower and thistle seeds there.

Already, the males have lost the brilliant gold coats that give them two of their many nicknames—"wild canary" and "shiner"—but they are still beautiful, the bold, intricate pattern of their black-and-white folded wings reminiscent of southwest Native American pottery. They announce their arrival at our bird feeders with loud, ascending "sweeet, sweeet" calls. To the scientists who originally gave them their species name, *tristis*, which means "sad," those calls sounded plaintive.

Both the male and female are usually peaceful but persistent guests at the feeders, unlike their close relatives, the pine siskins, which successfully threaten birds twice their size. American goldfinches give the impression of being "above the fray," often remaining to feed when other bird species swirl off in fright. I have seen a single goldfinch surrounded by fifteen quarreling house finches on the feeder, the goldfinch calmly and methodically eating while the house finches joust like miniature bantam roosters.

Bradford Torrey, writing in 1885, described the American goldfinch as "one of the loveliest of birds. With his elegant plumage, his rhythmical, undulatory flight, his beautiful song, and his most beautiful soul, he ought to be one of the best beloved.... He is always cheerful ... and always amiable."[1] In his day, Torrey thought that goldfinches were not as appreciated as they might have been. He would probably be pleased to know that the American goldfinch has since been honored as the state bird of Washington, New Jersey, and Iowa. And many feeder owners care enough about the species to spend the extra money for tube feeders and thistle seeds specifically as lures of goldfinches. In fact, their genus name, *Carduelis,* is Latin for "thistle." And another of their nicknames, "thistle-bird," attests to their liking for those seeds.

Walter P. Nickell, a researcher who studied 264 American goldfinch nests in Michigan from 1933 until 1949, believed that the clearing of land throughout the goldfinches' range by settlers increased goldfinch populations, since the birds prefer open habitat, particularly in riparian woodlands. Unlike many bird species, American goldfinches seem to have benefited rather than suffered from humanity's actions. "Panoplied in jet and gold," as one ornithologist described them, American goldfinches are one of the most charming residents of our mountaintop.[2] And I was glad today to find so many feeding on the abundant wild foods in preference to my feeder offerings.

NOVEMBER 9. There still has been no appreciable rain, despite occasional lowering clouds. With the clear-cutting of the mountainside continuing, we made the decision to post our property against hunting for the first time since we have lived here. Should even one hunter drop a lighted

1. As cited in Bent, *Life Histories of North American Cardinals* ..., p. 447.
2. Frank Chapman, as quoted in E. H. Forbush and John Richard May, *Natural History of the Birds of Eastern and Central North America,* p. 498.

match or cigarette by mistake, the mountain and we would go up in smoke because of the highly incendiary piles of slash everywhere.

But we have other legitimate reasons for posting too. Already the wildlife has been disturbed by the cutting and needs some respite from harassment at this time of year. Also, we have learned from bitter experience that we cannot judge the law-abiding hunters from the outlaws. Because we are so close to town and because all the neighboring land is posted, we have been getting more and more hunters every year. By posting, we can decide who we will and will not allow on our land. Furthermore, since our land almost totally encloses our neighbor's, our posting will keep their land hunter-free too. So, with the help of four hunting friends whom we trust, Bruce has started the arduous job of stapling up hundreds of signs along the boundaries of our 500 acres.

Deer streamed up and down Sapsucker Ridge and the upper end of First Field just after sunrise as we sat eating breakfast, a sure sign that the woods were full of wild turkey hunters this lovely Saturday. I also spotted a sharp-shinned hawk sitting on a tree branch along the driveway.

The drummer was on his log and drumming, and I scared up several more grouse out along the Far Field Trail. Pileated woodpeckers were loudly vocal, especially in the woods around the house and in the Far Field Road woods. Otherwise, it was silent. There were too many people in the woods, so the animals and birds stayed hidden.

NOVEMBER 10. I walked along Laurel Ridge Trail this lovely Sunday and was startled when a small black bear suddenly took off from where it had been lying under a laurel bush. All I had was a glimpse of a large, black, hairy rear end in full flight, but I found the imprint of where it had rested. Could that be the same bear that marked the locust tree at the Far Field?

Now that most of the leaves are down and the color gone, I am recompensed by the light of late fall and winter. It pours down on me in the open woods, a benediction and a promise, casting an aura over what most people think of as dull colors—beige, brown, gray, and black. But then nature's way with color is far superior to humanity's poor imitations. Consider how lovely the green of fields and trees are against a deep blue sky, yet those colors in a dress or a room often clash. The same is true of the orange, dark red, and wine colors of autumn leaves—spectacularly harmonious outside, nerve-jangling inside—probably because such colors must be lit by direct sunlight to attain an inner glow. Electric light or sunlight shining through windows will not do the trick.

Along the Far Field Trail, I found a few birds—white-breasted nuthatches, black-capped chickadees, cedar waxwings. Mostly though, the sounds were made by the wind rattling dry leaves like old bones, shaking off the last of life in preparation for the long, cold sleep ahead. Finally, later in the day, the rain began and fell, more or less continuously, throughout most of the night.

NOVEMBER 11. Snow mixed with rain, but still the loggers came and worked through the miserable weather all day. What will it take to drive them off the mountain, along with their obscene machines? Whatever it is, I wish it would come soon.

Despite the weather, I held my first FeederWatch of the season this morning. I am an enthusiastic veteran of this project, launched jointly by the Cornell Laboratory of Ornithology and the Long Point Bird Observatory in Ontario in 1987 to count birds at bird feeders across the continent during the winter months. As a member of the

Laboratory of Ornithology, I learned about the program through their newsletter. Thousands of birdwatchers were also recruited through pleas in other bird-related media. By November 14, 1987, I and 2,148 other birdwatchers from every state in the United States and most Canadian provinces were armed with computerized data sheets and easy-to-understand instructions. We were to count the greatest numbers and species of birds at our feeders at any one time for two consecutive days every other week from then until April 1. In order not to skew the statistics, we were to choose our count days ahead of time and then stick to them no matter what the weather or the number of birds at the feeder on those days. Since the main objective is to get an index of bird abundance, what we don't see is as important as what we do see, and if the birds are not there, they want to know that too.

The entire count period does include two whole days, morning and afternoon, but it does not mean that I must stay glued in place all that time. I usually spend the first two or three hours of the first morning of my count seated in front of my kitchen window. After that, I go about my other work but continue to look out the window frequently throughout both days of the count. If the first day is mild and the second snowy, I'll spend more time watching on the second day since I know bad weather brings in the birds.

Participants also record both the high and low daylight temperatures for each count period, the percentage of cloud-cover, wind speed and duration, and snow cover. Another form, which is read by people, not computers, is filled out only once each season and asks for a description of the feeding area, the types and numbers of feeders, and the kinds and amount of food used. Still another form, to be sent in at the end of the count season, gives participants a chance to comment on the project, reporting unusual happenings and recording mammal species attracted by their feeders.

The ultimate aim of Project FeederWatch is to monitor bird populations, and each year they report intriguing fluctuations of whole groups of birds. My first year marked an enormous pine siskin irruption, the first we had ever had on the mountain. Two years later we had another, smaller one. Why, after sixteen years of no pine siskins, did we have two out of four winters when they were as common as dark-eyed juncos? What does it all mean? It means, as usual, that nature is never static and always interesting. Intriguing questions about winter bird populations keep me paying my money and signing up year after year.

So with today's miserable weather, the bird species and numbers increased as the day progressed, with up to nine American goldfinches at a time. But the house finches blanketed the feeder and the porch steps and gobbled the seed, driving off all but determined white-breasted nuthatches which thrust their rapier bills threateningly at the cheeky finches. Each nuthatch first descended from above, hanging from the feeder roof and then sliding down along the side to grab seeds. If that approach didn't chase away the finches, the nuthatch rushed around inside the feeder, beak pointed toward the finches. This neatly cleared off the invaders, almost like those swashbuckling movies of old when the hero, armed with his sword, cleaved a safe pathway with deft thrusts of his weapon. American goldfinches minded their own business, mixing physically with the house finches on the steps, but remaining psychically off in their own worlds as they calmly cracked open and ate seeds. They did not take alarm as quickly as the supernervous house finches whenever I appeared at the window. A pair of northern cardinals also fed, but they were even more nervous than the finches. Dark-eyed juncos persistently flew in and out and foraged on the steps and weeds below. They are also pushy birds, unlike the timid American tree sparrow that tried to feed as inconspicuously as possible far from the madding crowd below the steps. Later, when others join this lone bird and the group numbers five or ten, these sparrows will be as aggressive as the house finches and dark-eyed juncos.

When the feeder was filled with screaming, fighting house finches, black-capped chickadees and tufted titmice generally stayed away, but when there were fewer finches, they continued to fly in and out to snatch seed from under the finches' noses, so to speak. Otherwise, the chickadees and titmice preferred to use the tube feeder, which the house finches cannot dominate, or to snatch seed from the step. In the bird feeder world, at least, overwhelming numbers coupled with feisty, noisy personalities keep all lesser species (except the nuthatches) at bay.

Later, I took a walk in the sleet. The only action was along the Far Field Trail when two bucks appeared together and other deer scattered. Probably there were does in estrus nearby and the bucks were in pursuit or at least checking the scent signs. When I sat down, one buck actually sneaked past me. Obviously, ardor is dampening their usual caution. Bruce read a piece in the paper the other day about a buck that charged a hunter. The hunter, in desperation, grabbed and held on to the buck's antlers for six hours, he said, until his calls for help were finally heard. The buck continued to be combative and had to be destroyed. People speculated that he had been raised on a game farm and had not learned proper fear of humanity. So be careful, Bruce told me. But I laughed. It is humanity going amok that scares me, not wildlife.

NOVEMBER 12. Tundra swans were heading south at nine o'clock this morning. First seventy flew over in a perfect V formation. The second V was lopsided with two much smaller birds, probably Canada geese, at one end. The swans continued to sweep over the mountain in larger and larger flocks most of the morning, their bodies gleaming white despite the weak sunshine.

Later I went walking to the Far Field thicket to look for more bird action, and I found it. In answer to my "pishing," a rufous-sided towhee called "chewink" twice—setting an even later record for towhees on the mountain. White-throated sparrows sang, dark-eyed juncos flushed from the underbrush, Carolina wrens, northern cardinals, and tufted titmice scolded. Twenty-seven cedar waxwings sat calling from high in the tallest tree. Fifteen more landed in a tree near me that was draped in grapevines and were quickly joined by the twenty-seven. Then they all lost their nerve because of my closeness and swirled back into the tallest tree. From there many flew to another nearby treetop laden with grape-covered vines where they fed with dark-eyed juncos and white-throated sparrows, bossily supervised by a loud-mouthed Carolina wren. Three common grackles flew in but were quickly driven of. Eventually, the waxwings flew away too, leaving the grapes to the juncos and sparrows.

I returned through the Far Field, looking for migrating songbirds. There I found a flock of white-throated sparrows scratching for seeds underneath the weeds. As I pushed my way closer to watch them, I was almost immediately rewarded with a rarer sighting. A small flock of fox sparrows flew up from the ground where they had been hidden by dried goldenrod. Since they are shy, retiring birds they gave me only glimpses of their foxy red tails, rusty-streaked breasts, and gray and reddish brown heads and necks before flying back down into the underbrush. But I continued flushing those largest members of the sparrow tribe because I was eager to get a better look at them.

Watching a fox sparrow flock was a treat. Usually I only see them singly during spring migration when one drops in for a scratch among the feeder seeds en route to its summer breeding grounds in the conifers, thickets, and shrubs of Newfoundland, the Magdalen Islands, or southern Labrador. Although the fox sparrow (*Passerella iliaca*) is endemic to North America from the Atlantic to the Pacific, and from the southern U.S. border northward to Canada's tree line, bird banding studies show that in the East, the largest breeding population lives in Newfoundland and their favorite wintering spot is North Carolina. To get from one place to the other they use the Atlantic flyway.

They are almost exclusively vegetarians, except when they are raising three to five young in the summer, and they particularly like wild fruits and the seeds of such unpopular weeds as ragweed and smartweed. Fox sparrows have been observed associating with song sparrows, rufous-sided towhees, dark-eyed juncos, and American tree sparrows, but the times I have seen them here they have been accompanied by white-throated sparrows.

Someday I am hoping to hear their song, which one researcher described as "utterly unsparrowlike, a unique performance that seems not in the least akin to bird music, but more like the soft tinkling of silver bells."[3] Although like most birds, their best singing is done on their breeding grounds, fall singing for short periods has been recorded between October 30 and November 23. But they were silent today as they searched for food among the withered growth of tall weeds.

When I finally returned home, a common raven flew over the house "cronking." And late in the day, a doe and

3. S. D. Judd, as quoted in Bent, *Life Histories of North American Cardinals* . . . , p. 140b.

her two fawns came up the slope to within ten feet of the back porch to forage on pokeberries. The doe seemed transfixed as she stopped to watch dark-eyed juncos fly in and out from the ground below the bird feeder. One of her fawns was still fuzzy looking and very small, almost like a stuffed animal, but it seemed healthy enough.

I was awakened several times in the middle of the night by creatures scrambling in the walls behind the headboard of my bed. The "wild life" in an old house continues even in the wee hours, creating a subculture I have never seen but can only imagine—mice playing, eating, procreating, dying.

NOVEMBER 13. Thirty-three degrees, cool, damp, and gray with occasional spits of rain in the air and a steady wind, but still the rampage continued in the hollow. I've given up hope that anything will be left. The cutting is a continual, nagging pain to me that I cannot excise except by walking as far away from it as possible, so I was off by mid-morning for the Far Field.

One buck dashed in front of me on Laurel Ridge Trail near the powerline right-of-way. I "pished" up a flock of black-capped chickadees, a downy woodpecker, and a brown creeper further along the trail. At the Far Field, a flock of dark-eyed juncos flew in, but the thicket, wrapped in the silence of November, was empty of birds today.

So I walked back by way of First Field to check on the American bittersweet crop. Several years ago Bruce first discovered it twining up among the bare branches of a wild black cherry tree at the edge of the field. I had been searching for it for years during November but had been unsuccessful. Yet once Bruce spotted it across the width of the field—its red fruits shining brightly against the gray, leafless tree branches—we wondered how we could have missed it for so long.

American bittersweet (*Celastrus scandens*) is a shrubby, climbing vine often reaching a height of twenty feet and is found along country roadsides near old walls, beside stream banks, in low thickets, and on hillsides. It has small, inconspicuous, greenish white flowers in June which are succeeded by clusters of loose, drooping, orange-colored, berrylike fruits near the end of summer. By November those globular capsules have split open and reveal the fleshy coated, bright scarlet seeds which are so attractive. The fruit hangs on all winter, and I have found both American robins and eastern bluebirds harvesting it early in March when little else is available for them to eat. For that reason, I am careful to cut only a few for my winter bouquets.

Today I found that the vines had spread to several trees and were heavy with clumps of seeds, the best crop I had ever seen here. So I clipped a few more than usual and filled two small vases, one for the sitting room desk and the other for the table.

NOVEMBER 14. I walked along the edge of the First Field slope this morning to catch the warmth and look for birds, but I saw nothing out of the ordinary, just the usual dark-eyed juncos, northern cardinals, black-capped chickadees, tufted titmice, and a Carolina wren. Then my attention was caught by a beautiful flowering witch hazel tree just above the bittersweet area. Its yellow blossoms shone against the blue sky.

Later, I ascended the Far Field Trail and spotted a buck's rear end before he spotted me. Quietly and carefully I sat down on the trail and watched him feeding. Finally he raised his head with its small, four-point rack and saw me. Slowly, deliberately, he stomped first one front hoof down and then the other before moving off, stiff-legged, over the ridgetop.

It continued to be a buck day because as I walked down First Field I saw two bucks chasing two does at the edge of the field, one buck snorting as it ran. Finally, crossing the field below the powerline right-of-way, I watched a six-point buck closely following a doe back and forth, his nose within five feet of her rear end, but she kept discreetly ahead of him until they both disappeared into the thick forest brush.

At 4:15 this afternoon two does grazed on the lawn. A four-point buck tried approaching them but they both shied away from him. Then he walked into the edge of First Field and sank down in the weeds near the pear tree sapling. Next, an eight-point buck came up the road and also approached both does, but they rejected him as well. After sniffing the does, he trotted off into the weeds directly toward where I thought the four-point buck was hiding. But the eight-point walked right past the area, and then the four-point appeared further up in the field, his head held submissively lower than the dominant eight-point. His lack of panic showed in his ambling gait. The eight-point ignored him and stalked past nearby. Both continued on up the field while the does remained placidly eating on the lower lawn.

NOVEMBER 15. Just as I was getting ready to go walking this morning, a beautiful eight-point buck came down into the flat area beneath the house to sniff the air. He kept looking around. Then he stared down toward the powerline right-of-way. He didn't even glance toward the house.

Through my binoculars, his forehead fur looked orange brown and matted. He had a striking white bib, white above his nose, and he seemed to weep white beneath his eyes, conveying an impression of kindly calmness. He turned around, started to forage, but peered down the hollow road instead. One ear flipped back and forth. Finally, he turned and looked behind him, then walked back up into the woods almost to the Short Way Trail before trying to forage while still keeping a watch around him.

Again he turned and trotted purposefully back down to the flat area to graze on the still-green grass. Suddenly, he started pawing the ground. Two does appeared, coming from the direction of the powerline right-of-way with their heads down. He took off after one up the slope, and they disappeared into the woods just as someone called me on the phone to ask why we were posting our land!

A few minutes later while I was down in the guest-house, I glanced out the window to see the same buck walking past the old Kiefer pear tree at eye level and only about twenty feet away. He paused, looked carefully at the window, walked nervously around the area, and then trotted down the hill across First Field. When I left the guest-house, I heard, but did not see, a deer snort from down the driveway. Then, as I walked up Guest House Trail, I surprised a large doe that stood frozen in the middle of the trail. Finally she snorted and ran up the trail ahead of me, veering off into the woods and out of sight. I'm beginning to feel like a voyeur where white-tailed deer are concerned.

NOVEMBER 16. At the edge of the Far Field I sat and watched a fox squirrel gathering mouthfuls of fallen leaves to add to a winter nest it was building in the crotch of a black cherry tree. The squirrel had used live grapevines to form its foundation. During the time I sat there, I counted six collecting trips by the squirrel, all taking the identical path: down the cherry tree to a broken tree branch sticking up at a right angle to the nest tree, then halfway down that branch to a standing snag, and from there to the forest floor. It took the squirrel only a few seconds each time to cram a mass of dried leaves in its mouth and then to repeat the same measured trip in reverse back up to the nest. The squirrel always slid in behind the nest mass, so I couldn't actually see if it was adding to that nest or stuffing the material into a hidden hole in the back of the trunk. Finally I walked around the back of the nest tree for a closer look. As I stood there, the fox squirrel emerged from behind the leaf mass and started down its regular route until it spotted me. Then it went the opposite way, leaping onto nearby tree trunks and down to the forest floor, disappearing from sight for several minutes. Finally, it returned and climbed a nearby tree to scold me loudly. I remained seated, so it again leaped away. Nevertheless, I was pleased to have found the home of a fox squirrel and looked forward to watching it throughout the winter months.

According to Joseph F. Merritt in his *Guide to the Mammals of Pennsylvania,* gray and fox squirrels construct similar nests, either utilizing old woodpecker holes, which they stuff with leaves, or building outside leaf nests such as the one I observed. Fox squirrels may build their leaf nests anywhere from ten to fifty feet above the ground, constructing them of leaves, grass, and roots with a framework of twigs. Merritt says that nests range from about twelve to twenty inches in their outside diameter and have an inner cavity diameter of between six and eight inches. The squirrels always enter by a hole in the side of the nest adjacent to the tree trunk, which is why I had so much difficulty in determining exactly where the fox squirrel was emerging. And the nest I watched was thirty feet from the ground, too high for me to see that back entrance. Since a fox squirrel can build such a nest in less than twelve hours, it was probably nearly finished when I appeared in mid-afternoon. Shortly afterward, it started sleeting with occasional heavy snow, which drove me home for the day and the fox squirrel, presumably, into the shelter of its waterproof winter nest.

NOVEMBER 17. Oh, peaceful Sunday when the mountain can rest from the takers, both loggers and hunters. We walked through our own intact woodlands, happy to know that the big trees here will not be cut down in their prime, at least not while we own the property.

In the afternoon I lay near the top of First Field in the light and silence, hearing only the occasional drone of a plane overhead or a train whistle in the valley. It was like lying in an enormous bowl because of the encircling ridges of trees above me. I felt protected and watched over by the fierce eye of the sun, which cast its brilliant light over the field, glazing the dried grasses and goldenrod with a sheen of silvery beige. Finally, I rose reluctantly when the shadows started to slip over the field and wended my way back down to the house, cleansed in spirit as no church was ever able to cleanse me.

Much later, as I was settling into bed for the night, I heard a loud bang downstairs and thought it was Steve coming up to say something, but no light went on and no voice was raised in question. Another bang, again like a door slamming, so I crept down the stairs through the moonlit sitting room and into the kitchen. I peered out the back door window and saw a big bear lying on the back porch, its back turned toward me. It looked as if it were moonbathing.

Quickly and quietly I zipped back upstairs to arouse Bruce. He rushed down, took one look out the window, and went running to get his camera. In the meantime, I watched as the bear stood up from the mass of birdseed it had been lying in, having overturned the garbage can of birdseed earlier, and reached up to tilt the bird feeder. Somehow, standing a few feet away from a three-hundred-pound black bear with only two flimsy doors between us was not altogether reassuring. It shuffled about and sniffed the other garbage cans, but did not touch them since they held only well-washed bottles and cans ready for recycling. And it didn't seem too fond of the seeds since it ignored the other two cans of birdseed.

Bruce finally returned without his camera since he had only black and white film in it, although I was not sure what difference color would have made on a moonlit night anyway. Running for his camera had just been a reflex action on his part, I think. As we both stood quietly watching, the bear wandered off the porch, walked up the sloping bulkhead cellar door, and peered into the sitting room through the bow window, its nose nearly touching the glass. Bruce peered back at it, his nose almost pressed against the window, and said, "Go away."

"Woof, woof," the bear replied. There we stood at an impasse, the bear staring in at us, we staring out at it for several long minutes, before it finally wandered off in the direction of the trash burner. Then Bruce stepped out onto the back porch and yelled and hooted at the bear who "woofed" in reply, the sounds floating back through the darkness. This bluffing went on for a couple of minutes until Bruce was almost certain that the bear had moved off. He hoped, by such an unfriendly reception, to persuade the animal that our yard was not a good place to be and that we did not have available food for it.

It took us both a long time to get back to sleep, wondering whether the bear would return and this time come right into the kitchen to help itself. But it didn't. Had the bear been an experienced panhandler or just curious? Remembering how shortsighted bears are and how it would not have been able to smell us through the wall, I imagine it was trying hard to see what we were when it peered into the bow window. Or maybe it had just been curious. Whatever its intentions had been, its unauthorized visit had been the closest and longest encounter we have had with a black bear.

NOVEMBER 18. At dusk, the house was surrounded by deer, and I went from window to window, trying to keep up with the action outside. A doe and two fawns wandered up the hillside. They seemed alert as they paused to sniff and look around near the back porch, but they were clearly ill-at-ease and kept moving. A few minutes later the eight-point buck looked into my back kitchen window, sniffed around, glanced at the doe and fawns feeding in the side yard, and then minced off toward the back of the garage.

Next, I spotted two more bucks—a six- and a four-point—in the flat area. The four-point actually had the larger rack, so the six-point retreated into the woods while the four-point paced along the ditch and raised his head to reach hanging apple tree branches and then mountain laurel leaves, but he seemed to be marking them rather than feeding on them. Finally, he too disappeared just as a doe and her fawn emerged from the grape tangle and stood under the lantern post fifteen feet from the back kitchen window. There they stopped to engage in what looked like an ecstatic licking session. Those two never did mingle with the three in the side yard that had settled down to serious eating. When I turned on the spotlights, the deer spooked off, but there is no doubt that our yard is *the* place for bucks to look over does, the deer equivalent of "Standing on the Corner, Watching All the Girls Go By."

NOVEMBER 19. The skidders came bursting over the ridge at their usual time, catching me, as always, in the pit of my stomach. The loathsome creatures proceeded to claw away at the dead logs, sending a din over the peaceful mountain.

So I fled to the Far Field where I was greeted by the call of an eastern bluebird and an American robin, followed by a pair of soaring common ravens. But the stars that stayed to entertain me were a dozen foraging, calling black-capped chickadees in the weeds, a pileated woodpecker looking over a black locust grove of tempting trunks, a female northern cardinal that landed and scolded overhead, and a huge, beautiful fox squirrel that materialized from the tangle of breast-high field weeds and climbed halfway up a locust tree, pausing, as if on cue, to wave its banner tail.

The pileated woodpecker trumpeted loudly and flashed its white wings as it flew from tree to tree. Another pileated, probably its mate, yelled from the opposite end of the field. Three American goldfinches flew in to land and call and feed on black birch cones. American crows cawed, more American robins "tut-tutted" their arrival, tufted titmice scolded, and downy woodpeckers called and tapped politely in sharp contrast to the continual raucous noises of the pileateds. All the while the sun winked in and out as I watched the action.

Then, almost as suddenly as they had arrived, they were gone. The players had left the stage abruptly and moved on to other forums. But I could still hear them off in the wings, speaking in backstage whispers.

NOVEMBER 20. It warmed quickly into a hazy, Indian summer day. In the flat area, a six-point buck stood still and looked fixedly up at the house. At first I thought he was watching birds at the feeder and, to some extent, he was because whenever they flew off in a flurry, he looked up from his eating.

A doe and her fawn fed nearby, but he ignored them and kept lifting his head and sniffing. While the fawn followed several feet behind him as if curious, he paced around, still looking up at the house. It was then that I spotted a doe a short distance down in the grape tangle, hidden by the brush, her twitching ears giving her location away. After several more minutes of eating and being followed by the curious fawn, which then sat down nearby and gazed fixedly at the buck as if in hero-worship, the buck suddenly took off after a running doe, heading up into Laurel Ridge woods where I lost him. I thought at first the doe was the fawn's mother, but she and her fawn stood up in the weeds of the flat area, and the doe that had been hiding in the grape tangle was gone. She must have dashed off in the few brief moments I had taken to write notes about my observations.

By early afternoon it was seventy-one degrees, and I walked down Laurel Ridge to see what I could see across to the Sapsucker Ridge side of the hollow where the loggers were working. What I saw was a stocky, middle-aged man in a white tee shirt cutting down a huge tree, trimming it, and then hauling it off with the orange skidder up the Lower Road. It looked as if they were beginning to decimate the one area that had not been touched yet. From halfway down Laurel Ridge, it was not very far across to where they were working.

What a sea of fallen trees and what a depressing view I had. Those lumbermen are no Paul Bunyans, huge and brawny, cutting trees by using their own brute strength. It is their big machines that give them the power to destroy the natural world. Such destruction, by the "third chimpanzee," as scientist Jared Diamond calls us in his book of the same name, has rendered nature impotent.

There are other ways to treat the land, to respect its integrity, to protect its biodiversity, and still to make judicious use of what it freely offers us. But few landowners have the patience to wait for slower profits. Or the opportunity to work with reasonable woodsmen like Bob Taber and his son Dewayne, who live and work in the Ozark Mountains. They use teams of horses and mules to drag out the selectively cut trees they log for discriminating timber owners who do not want skidders in their woods. With such a setup they don't have to clear logging trails, and, as Taber told George Laycock in an *Audubon* magazine article, "They [skidders] ride all over the little stuff three and four inches thick and that's our future timber. Why, log skidders will ride down trees big as a stovepipe." Surprisingly, Taber and his son work less and make more money than the big-time loggers in their area who are in debt for the skidders they buy and their commitments to the mill that purchases their timber. And they have far more work than they can ever do because of their careful methods. Such methods enable them to come back to the same woodlot every ten years and harvest mature trees for the landowner, yet leave a healthy woods complete with wildflowers and wild creatures.

Although even the U.S. Forest Service opposes such low-impact logging now, many far-sighted foresters see that kind of logging as the wave of the future. But change will only take place if people insist on kinder treatment of both private and public forests and if we admit that while we will continue to need wood, we will have to harvest it in ways that will not severely impact the land. Otherwise, as with all the natural resources we have recklessly squandered in what at first seemed to be a continent of unlimited riches, we will be left with a vastly diminished ecosystem producing, if we are lucky, factory trees on barren plantations. Gone will be the wildflowers, birds, wild animals, amphibians, reptiles, shrubs, and even insects which comprise the delicate ecosystem we are all a part of.

NOVEMBER 21. The last of the migrants are gone now, leaving only those birds which can survive on the meager winter foods our woods and fields offer them. Some birds, such as the American tree sparrows and dark-eyed juncos, migrate from the north and stop here, spending between six and seven months on the mountain. That, according to the latest ornithological thinking, makes them "our" birds along with all the species that remain here the year around.

By the same token, those birds whose arrival we eagerly await each spring—the swallows and warblers, thrushes and flycatchers—are not "our" birds but belong to the tropics where they spend over six months of the year. We should think of their time with us as a summer vacation, the experts tell us.

I doubt if the birds would agree with that since they perform their most important functions—the courting, mating, and raising of their families—in the north and would probably consider, as we do, that "home is where the heart is." Nevertheless, their time in the south is no vacation either because obtaining food in competition with the permanent residents can be difficult. In fact, the migrants often change not only their food preferences but their behavior patterns in order to survive.

Their arrival in the Antilles, Mexico, Central America, and northern South America crowd the year-round bird residents. Most of the migrants either disperse themselves widely or concentrate in smaller areas. Those which are widely dispersed are generally territorial and defend an area only for themselves, not for a mate and family as they do in the north. They also forage in uncut rain forests where insect food is the most plentiful. Northern waterthrushes, which spend the winter in Venezuela, vigorously defend their own plots, as do many of the other warblers that do not change their plumage in the fall such as American redstarts and yellow-throated warblers.

Those warblers that do change to duller colors, Blackburnians and bay-breasteds, for instance, often join native flocks of birds and do not defend territories. Still others—golden-winged, blue-winged, and worm-eating warblers—keep their bright colors and defend these mixed flocks as they would territories. They specialize in probing for insects in curled-up leaves. Since this requires strict attention, the individual warblers cannot watch as carefully for predators. Instead they depend on the flock for a warning.

Many migrant birds change their eating habits completely during the winter months. Some yellow-throated warblers stay around the lights of resort hotels on the Yucatan peninsula searching for insects rather than foraging in their customary habitat of open woodlands. Broad-winged hawks, which winter in Amazonia, become crepuscular since they feed almost exclusively on large, dusk-loving katydids rather than on the small birds, reptiles, and mammals they eat here. Cape May warblers change from eating insects to sucking the juices and nectar of fruits growing in the West Indies, using a tubular tongue they have evolved for the purpose. American robins, too, are fruit eaters in Mexico, where they form large sociable flocks just as those do that winter on our mountain, eating wild grapes and Hercules' club berries. Baltimore orioles also flock and feed on the nectar of flowering trees in Panama, forming large roosts at dusk.

Except for the woodpeckers, nuthatches, and brown creepers which get their food from tree insects, most of the birds that successfully winter here also flock. I never see just one black-capped chickadee or American goldfinch or golden-crowned kinglet or tufted titmouse in the winter woods, and visitors like purple finches or common redpolls usually arrive as part of a mixed species flock. If a song sparrow or field sparrow winters, it usually joins other small birds. The lone bird, a gray catbird or rufous-sided towhee, for instance, which occasionally winters in this area has a harder time of it and often perishes before the end of the season unless it finds a well-stocked bird feeder.

So "our" birds—the year-rounders, the northern migrants, the few strays—must also be adaptable, just as the migrants to the tropics are. That, after all, is the key to survival in this changeable natural world of ours.

NOVEMBER 22. Late fall is a good time to hunt for bracket fungi. Once the leaves are down and the vistas are wide, it is easy to wander through the woods at a leisurely pace, examining dead snags and fallen trees where the bracket fungi grow. Such a peaceful pastime can be carried out on even the darkest days because most of the bracket fungi I find are white, a striking contrast to the gray tree trunks. Others, though, can be beige or sulphurous yellow or even striped with varying shades of gray and brown. Some have long, velvety hairs on their surfaces; others have a dazzling variety of colors and textures of their undersides. Most are half-moon shaped, but some are round and still others are highly irregular.

Bracket fungi, in other words, are as interesting, varied, and colorful as their relatives, the common mushrooms. Unlike them, however, many bracket fungi are perennial, and their fruiting bodies, called conks, persist for several seasons. But they do live and reproduce like other mushrooms. Once it matures, the conk produces spores which land on wood and, if conditions are right, small threadlike strands, called mycelia, grow and penetrate into the wood.

Enzymes produced by the mycelia are able to break down the wood cells and provide nourishment for the fungus.

Some bracket fungi can utilize most of the wood, and because they leave it white, spongy, and fibrous are called "white rots." Others only use the cellulose of wood cells and leave the wood brown and crumbly. Appropriately enough, those are the "brown rots."

Bracket fungi can be either parasitic (living on live, mature trees) or saprophytic (living on decay, debris, or dead matter). For a long time the notorious ones, such as those which cause Dutch elm disease, led people to believe that all bracket fungi were harmful. In reality, they are necessary to the cyclic growth of the forest since they combine with bacteria and microscopic animals to break down the debris in the forest and release the nutrients needed by living plants.

Searching for bracket fungi forces me to move slowly and examine every tree trunk, living or dead. Today I found a great variety of them, all of which were growing on dead trees. The most attractive were *Polyporus versicolor* which produces fanlike rows of multicolored rings on fallen logs. Sometimes they grow in whorls at the end of the logs, hence their common nickname, "turkey tails." With their varying shades of gray, brown, beige, and off-white, they seemed to be aptly named.

On one large snag I found *Ganoderma applanatum*—tough, thick, half-moon shaped bracket fungi ranging in color from light brown to off-white. Their undersides were smooth and brownish white. Sometimes artists draw pictures on them, which accounts for their common name, "artist's conk." The largest of bracket fungi, they can grow more than two feet in diameter and live fifty years.

The third bracket fungi I identified was *Polyporus hirsutus*, a common, hardwood-loving species that is covered with dense small hairs and shows concentric zones of gray. Identification for many of the more nondescript, white species was difficult, so instead of identifying them, I was content to merely admire them.

Hunting for bracket fungi in a cold November woods can be rewarding in other ways. Several times I surprised herds of deer, and twice I flushed a ruffed grouse. In a wild grape tangle I stopped to watch a flock of white-throated sparrows foraging. Eventually, a light patter of rain and a cold wind sent me scurrying home to warm my November-chilled bones and drink a cup of coffee. Oh yes! and to rejoice that the steady rain had driven the loggers off. And so I blessed the rain and prayed for more.

NOVEMBER 23. Another Saturday and I spent a portion of it reclining against the Far Field Road bank, listening to the sounds or lack of sounds around me. I quickly established the fact that a turkey hunter sat up over the hill because I could hear him scraping his turkey call at infrequent intervals.

Below me the rustle in the woods signaled the presence of a browsing doe and her fawn. Loud calling from the same vicinity was made by a hairy woodpecker. Mostly, though, the woods were quiet, and I could hear each light breath of wind that moved through and rattled the dead leaves still clinging to the treetops. Other sounds, which had nothing to do with the mountain and which I have learned to block out for the most part—high-flying jet planes, train whistles, truck traffic, and the rattle of farm machinery—made little impact on me today since the major noise, the logging operation, was stilled for the weekend.

The late naturalist and writer Hal Borland once said, in his book *Hill Country Harvest*, that he distinguished between silence, which he called a total lack of sound, and quiet. "Quiet," he wrote, "is the relative absence of the noise of machines, but it is also the lack of loud human voices."

Certainly, I rarely hear other human voices, and when I am home I have no television to turn on, no radio to listen to, no record player to operate. I like quiet. It enables me to hear what is going on in my mountain world. Whenever I step outside, I stop to listen before I look. Then I know which direction to glance in order to see the noisemaker. Often the creatures are hidden from me, but I can still have an inkling of what is happening if I listen.

On my way back from the Far Field Road bank, I heard American crows harassing a common raven near First Field. Within a few minutes the raven floated down along the ridgetop, croaking disgruntledly. Instantly the crows dispersed, their job done for the day. I also listened to ruffed grouse drumming along the Laurel Ridge Trail.

Best of all, though, was the scrambling sound I heard in the living room after dinner. I knew what it was because we have had such visitors before—a flying squirrel in the Franklin stove. With the fire screen in place, I carefully eased open the doors on the stove, and sure enough, a flying squirrel pressed itself against the screen. I pulled on a heavy work glove and slipped my hand around the screen, but the squirrel quickly burrowed down into last year's cold ashes. After a good deal of maneuvering, I firmly grasped the small, big-eyed creature and carried it out to the veranda where I set it on the arm of the wooden rocker. The squirrel glided down to the cement floor, scampered onto the lawn, and disappeared into the night.

NOVEMBER 24. Occasional snow flurries alternated with infrequent patches of blue sky and sunshine this windy day. One pileated woodpecker was abroad and called loudly as it flew above me. But mostly the woods

were silent again. On such a day I am reduced to elemen-
tals—sky, wind, creaking trees, rattling leaves—with only
the faint call of a common raven off in the whiteness.
Since most of the birds and animals are under cover on
such a day, I look for signs of their passing instead.

For instance, in the top corner of First Field I discovered that ten black locust and five Norway spruce saplings
had been used as buck rubs. Immediately, I conjured up a
peaceful vision of all the bucks gathering there to polish
their racks and, at the same time, to enjoy the spectacular
view. More likely, though, this is a popular sparring place
for bucks, although true fights between bucks are rare.
Many times young bucks—one and a half to two and a
half years old—are just testing each other by banging
their antlers together. Fights do occur at the onset of
breeding season, when one mature buck invades another's
turf or a younger buck decides to challenge the dominant
buck and displace him. But by and large bucks do not have
to fight other bucks that belong to their own group. Since
they have been associating with one another all year, they
have already established dominance and each buck knows
his standing in the hierarchy. Even though I frequently see
more than one buck at a time in our yard during rutting
season, I have yet to see any sparring or fighting.

At the Far Field thicket I found more evidence of the
rutting season—several secondary scrapes littered with
deer tracks and feces. Again I conjured up a vision, this
one of bucks and does meeting here and pairing off, an
anthropomorphic idea totally at odds with what really
happens between bucks and does. Although does can be
choosy, they usually mate repeatedly with only one buck.
Two days before a doe is actually ready, she begins seeking
out a buck by leaving a trail of urine and pheromones.
While every buck in the area may track her down, usually
only the dominant buck, which drives off the others,

claims her by "tending" her until she comes into estrus. Then he may copulate with her anywhere from once or twice during her twenty-four hours of receptivity to many times (one researcher reported eight times during the day-time alone). Since most breeding is done at night, actual figures are hard to come by. Once her time is up, though, the buck heads off to find another receptive doe. During the sixty-day rutting season, a mature buck may breed with between four and twenty does. On the other hand, after her twenty-four-hour fling, assuming she has con-ceived, the doe has no more interest in bucks.

Whatever may be happening at the thicket when I am not there, or, more likely, at night, the thicket appeared lifeless today except for a merry band of black-capped chickadees, accompanied by a few tufted titmice, that came through. So, I took shelter beneath a fallen tree trunk wreathed in grapevines as snow began falling again.

NOVEMBER 25. Our worst fears have been confirmed. Our lawyer called to tell us that the lumberman's son-in-law contacted him and demanded that he tell us we *must* give him a key to the gate. The neighbor who has allowed them to build a road and cross his property for logging purposes has closed the road this week before buck season and for the two weeks of the season itself. They want to be able to use our road to ferry up men and equipment so they can continue their cutting, which, he told our attorney, will be done down to the hollow road.

Apparently, they had no intention of staying above the 200-foot zone, as they have promised us so often. Know-ing our feelings about the dangers to us from erosion and sliding, our lawyer urged us to file a motion requesting a court injunction to keep them 200 feet above the road; he has already prepared a draft for us to review.

It looks as if the lumberman has no concern about safe-guarding our only access to the outside world. And, of course, he has refused to help us maintain the road even while claiming his right to use it whenever it suits him. Once again we have been too gullible and willing to believe the best about him and his operation. But it has been difficult to sort out who, in fact, is directing the activity— the lumberman, his son, or his son-in-law. Is the son-in-law following the lumberman's orders or not? During this whole operation the lumberman, so far as we can tell, has not visited the site even once but has been leaving the work to his son and son-in-law. The son-in-law's overbearing manner toward our attorney sounds to us like a bluff to cow us into giving them a key to the gate. Still hoping that the lumberman himself might agree to compromise or even negotiate with us, and convinced that he is not fully aware of what is going on, Bruce told our attorney that we would wait a bit longer before going into court. At least we will have over three weeks of peace before the neighbor opens up his road to them again.

I dragged myself to the top of First Field, depressed by the whole lumbering mess. But the view was glorious—a silver and blue day with a faint blush of rose. From there the world looked beautiful, the mountain untouched. And even though we seem to be losing to the rapine forces in this area, on the national front there has been some tempering of the "business at any cost" mentality. The Arctic National Wildlife Refuge has been saved from oil drilling, at least for now (1991). Several White House scientists have resigned over the administration's proposal to gut the federal wetland regulations and have leaked their own disastrous predictions of what the White House proposals would do to the few remaining wetlands in this country. Their report not only agreed with the environmentalists' assessments but was even more condemnatory. In other words, environmentalists had erred on the side of conservatism. Although the politicians and the business community, for the most part, may not care about such things, ordinary citizens and well-informed scientists do. Maybe there is hope for humanity's survival after all.

NOVEMBER 26. Looking for proof that the lumbermen would be back, I walked over our neighbor's property yesterday in search of skidders and bulldozers and found neither. The huge piles of cut logs were gone, and it looked as if they were finished. Surely there was nothing left to cut. It looked as if the son-in-law's threat to cut down to the road was just that. The Lower Road is completely blocked by fallen snags and piles of slash, so how could they use it to log the 200-foot zone? Bringing back all the equipment and re-clearing the roads would be a waste of time and money, especially since winter is almost here.

Meanwhile, the peaceful days in the hollow are like a balm. Even the occasional noise from the limestone quarry in the valley seems like nothing after the relentless screams of skidders. As usual, I headed along the same trails, eager not to miss the changes that occur along this familiar way. I've always felt a little guilty about this, however. Wasn't such an adherence to the same paths proof of my unadventurous spirit?

Then, not long ago, I read *Signs and Seasons* by the nineteenth-century naturalist John Burroughs. In it I found ample justification for what I have been doing the last twenty years. "The place to observe nature is where you are," he wrote. "The walk to take today is the walk you took yesterday. You will not find just the same thing: both the observed and the observer have changed" (p. 6).

So it was today when I was stopped by a convention of birds in the woods. I pass that way almost every day of the year, and occasionally I have startled a ruffed grouse there or have seen a small flock of birds in the vicinity. But never had I seen or heard so many birds at one time in that woodland patch.

I was forewarned by the whir of grouse wings and the snorts from a herd of deer that glided away into the laurel cover as I neared a grove of trees overhung by grapevines. I could hear the steady "plop-ploy" of grapes falling to the ground, evidently the sound that had lured the grouse and deer to the area.

Fifty American robins shook the vines with their plump bodies and filled the air with calling and singing. I sat down to watch them. They were soon joined by an equal number of evening grosbeaks which emitted their loud cries in between grape bites. The woods rang with their cacophonous calls, and this noise, in turn, began attracting other birds, some of which were not grape eaters.

Two pileated woodpeckers landed on a nearby tree and began hammering away in search of carpenter ants. Black-capped chickadees seemed interested in the insect larvae they found on grape clusters. Downy and hairy woodpeckers along with white-breasted nuthatches gleaned insects from tree bark.

But a red-bellied woodpecker and two male northern flickers jockeyed for positions on the vines and ate grapes as fast as the grosbeaks and robins. A flock of cedar waxwings joined the melee among the grapes, quickly followed by a dozen bouncing, whistling American goldfinches. By then the bird chorus had reached a crescendo of sound that almost overwhelmed my senses. I sat on and on, charmed by all I was seeing. A single white-throated sparrow sang, a counterpoint to the massed calls of the other birds. Tufted titmice and dark-eyed juncos also came winging in to kibitz with the others.

On a nearby tree I spotted a gray squirrel sitting and watching the birds. The squirrel and I were the only audience the birds had, not that they knew or cared about our interest. They had long ago forgotten the silent figure sitting at the base of a tree.

Eventually most of the birds dispersed, and I rose on cramped legs to make my way home. "I shall probably never see another such day . . . , because one can never exactly repeat his observation," Burroughs wrote, "cannot turn the leaf of the book of life backward, because each day has characteristics of its own."

NOVEMBER 27. Shall I sing of Indian summer, its warmth, its beauty, its rejuvenating spirit? What else but song can describe those wonderful halcyon days that occur periodically throughout November and, more recently, into December as well. Although statistically Indian summer is most likely to occur between November second and November sixth, lately the bouts of warm weather have continued sporadically until the winter solstice in mid-December. We *should* be having cold and wind, grayness and freezing rain. Instead we continue to have hazy, lazy days that keep me outside from dawn till dusk. It is, as Thoreau noted, the finest season of the year.

Why or when the phrase "Indian summer" first appeared has been the subject of dispute among scholars. Credit in most dictionaries is given to Major Ebenezer Denny, who wrote in his journal of October 13, 1794: "Pleasant weather. The Indian summer here. Frosty nights."[4] The "here" was LeBoeuf, near Erie, Pennsylvania, and encyclopedia entries identify western Pennsylvania as the place where the term originated. However, John Crevecoeur, author of *Letters from an American Farmer,* living in New York state, wrote in 1778 about "a short interval of smoke and mildness, called the Indian Summer."[5] And that is about as far back in literary time as the term can be traced.

4. Recounted in *The Oxford English Dictionary* (1970), vol. 5, p. 206.
5. Matthews, "The Term Indian Summer," pp. 19–28.

We do know that Indian summer became the most popular phrase in nineteenth-century writing to describe a weather phenomenon known for its haziness and high temperatures, which usually occurred after a harsh cold spell dubbed, in sexist terms, "squaw winter." By 1830 even Canadian and English writers had adopted the term.

But why "Indian summer?" Again, contradictory explanations have been offered. The most popular is that the haziness was caused by the smoke from Indian fires. Others claim that the term referred to the Indians' ability to predict such fine weather. Less charitable explanations deal with the Indians' character as seen through the eyes of the white men—Indian summer was as deceptive as the Indians themselves. Or, alternately, Indian summer was the last season of Indian attacks on white settlements. Finally, many people believe it was called Indian summer because the warm autumn weather was like a similar phenomenon the colonists had known in their countries of origin, but was just a little different in their new country, hence they attributed it to Native Americans or Indians as they were then called.

Fine spells of autumn weather have occurred and been noted in many northern countries since the days of the ancient Greeks. In Greek mythology such weather was considered a gift from the gods to the kingfisher, which they called "halcyon," from which our word for calm, peaceful weather originates. Kingfishers, they believed, built their nests floating on the sea about the time of the winter solstice and were able to charm the winds and sea into calmness until their families were reared—hence the "halcyon" or "kingfisher days" as they called them.

The English distinguish the warm days of October, which they call "St. Luke's summer," from the warm days of November, known as "St. Martin's summer." The Germans prefer the "summer of old women" and the French,

"St. Denis's summer." In Poland such a benign period of weather lasts three to four weeks and is referred to as "God's gift to Poland."

Meteorologists in this country can explain why the Indian summer phenomenon occurs. Warm air masses move northward from the Gulf of Mexico, causing a strong temperature inversion when they meet a cool, shallow, polar air mass. This anticyclone, as it is called, concentrates the smoke and dust in the air near the ground and also causes a large temperature variation between day and night.

Earlier this month, we had frosty nights, but for several days the temperature hovered between seventy and eighty degrees at midday. The bees were flying, the crickets still sang, and hundreds of mayflies danced in the sunlight. But now, even when it warms up, the insects are silent. Nevertheless, every warm day I am reminded of Nathaniel Hawthorne's words in *The American Notebooks* that describe "Indian summer days, with gentle winds, or none at all, and a misty atmosphere, which idealizes all nature, and a mild, beneficent sunshine, [which] invites one to lie down in a nook and forget all earthly care."[6]

I took his advice today, found a sheltered spot, and sunbathed, knowing that the days of warmth are fleeting. But I felt grateful for this day of reprieve, taking it as a special gift to be savored and remembered during the long, cold months of winter.

NOVEMBER 28. Ever since 1985 I have been participating in the Thanksgiving Bird Count held on Thanksgiving Day. An effort begun twenty years before by the Lynchburg Bird Club in Lynchburg, Virginia, it is cosponsored by the bird club and by the Carry Nature Sanctuary of

6. Ibid.

Sweet Briar College. The TBC seems to have been designed for the sedentary birdwatcher. In fact, in every way it is almost a parody of the much better known Christmas Bird Count. The CBC allows twenty-four hours of birding in a designated count circle fifteen miles in diameter. The TBC asks for one hour of focused attention on an area fifteen *feet* in diameter, preferably in your own backyard and encompassing your bird feeders. Both counts require participants to count all and every species within the time limit.

Every year the numbers who participate in the CBC increase and are now well over forty thousand. Those of us who are Thanksgiving Bird Counters hover in the five hundred to seven hundred range. Unlike the CBC, which allows groups to choose a count day within a designated time frame during the holiday season, the TBC requires an individual to count only on Thanksgiving Day. According to Dr. Ernest P. Edwards, who spearheads the effort, the count "began as a holiday 'game' but has evolved in such a way as to yield much useful information about bird populations and migratory movements. The emphasis is on fun for the participants, the satisfaction of being able to make a contribution to our knowledge of birds, and the accumulation of information that becomes more significant because it is gathered in the same way year after year."[7]

Surprisingly, despite the low number of participants, who are heavily skewed in the South and the East, comparisons with Project FeederWatch's eight thousand participants observing throughout late fall and winter indicate results closely similar to the TBC in both the common feeder species and the numbers of birds seen. Another surprise is that exactly the same species have

7. Quoted by Murphy, "Quick Takes," p. 6.

made up the top fifteen birds in the TBC every year since 1983, but that changes in position occur every year. And in 1990, for the first time, the Carolina wren made the list, tying for fifteenth place with the European starling. Further back in time, in 1976, the house finch overtook the purple finch in numbers, then they alternated with each other the following two years, and finally the house finch surged ahead, a position it has never relinquished.

Every year I compare my list with the TBC's top fifteen species. Their list has several of the same species that I record—black-capped chickadees, tufted titmice, northern cardinals, dark-eyed juncos, house finches, white-breasted nuthatches, American goldfinches, downy woodpeckers, and Carolina wrens—and several that I don't—blue jays, mourning doves, house sparrows, red-bellied woodpeckers, purple finches, and European starlings. But one of my most common species—the American tree sparrow—is never on their list.

So today, after putting the stuffed turkey in the oven, I settled down at 9:35 A.M. to begin my count; watching the feeder near the back porch. In the next hour I identified ten different species: a downy woodpecker, two white-breasted nuthatches, one male northern cardinal, three American tree sparrows, four tufted titmice, seven house finches, six dark-eyed juncos, two black-capped chickadees, a Carolina wren, and two pine siskins. But, as usual, all the other odd birds I've seen at the feeder this month (a fox sparrow, purple finches, song sparrows, and mourning doves) were absent, making the Thanksgiving Bird Count, on a smaller scale, as frustrating as the Christmas Bird Count. Where are all the birds when you need them?

NOVEMBER 29. Fifty-three degrees at dawn, overcast, with off and on dim sunshine and warming to sixty degrees by midday—still another bout of Indian summer. During the afternoon, I heard a steady volley of shots from a neighboring property, the ritual sighting in of rifles this day after Thanksgiving. Only two more days before buck season officially begins, and already I am tired of hunting. Ever since we posted our land, we have been besieged by telephone calls from hunters asking us why we have posted. While most have been understanding, a couple have been threatening. Still others have offered to pay us for the privilege of hunting on our land.

But one man's call did buoy my spirits. He said he had been up several weeks ago and had talked to the lumbering crew. "I watched them working for a while. Those guys are butchers." Apparently, although he was not a logger, some of his relatives were, so he knew a bad job when he saw it. And he understood and respected our reasons for posting the land.

I went walking along Laurel Ridge Trail and was stopped by a movement ahead which caught my attention. As I froze, a doe walked across the path, unconscious of my watching form. I heard another rustle from where she had emerged so I waited, expecting a yearling or two to come trailing after their mother. Instead, a large buck appeared in the open, seemingly intent on the doe's trail. Halfway across the path, however, he turned and, carefully balancing a well-formed, four-point rack, he walked slowly toward me. In the silence I could almost hear my quickened heartbeat. Surely he could see me standing there, I thought. But on he came. Visions of charging bucks flashed into my mind—stories I had read of tame, rutting bucks turning on their keepers and impaling them on their spikes. This fellow looked harmless, though, more as if he were sleepwalking. But in a few seconds he had advanced fifteen yards. I decided it was time to let him know I was there.

"What are you doing?" I asked quietly. But he kept coming, still slowly, head held high, looking straight at me.

"Don't you see me?" I persisted and then I shifted my weight so he could catch my movement. With that maneuver I stopped him a mere twenty yards from where I was standing. Swinging his head back and forth he peered intently in my direction. A sudden toss of his head, followed by a quiet snort, and then he turned slowly aside. In an unhurried trot, he headed off into the brush.

"Marvelous," I called after him, my tribute to his beauty and my thanks for the unforgettable moments he had just given me. And I wished him luck with the doe.

Later, at 4:45 P.M., after I had returned home, a sharp-shinned hawk landed on a post in the grape tangle. Magically, all the feeder birds had disappeared. The small hawk looked around for several seconds and then suddenly flew as straight (and as fast) as a bullet at the ten-foot-high juniper bush less than a foot in front of the house. It was stuffed full of dark-eyed juncos on their night perches. But not a junco was dislodged, and the sharpie flew off empty-taloned.

NOVEMBER 30. Tree-lovers, such as my husband and I, come into our own once the deciduous trees have lost their leaves. Only then can we appreciate the true height and majesty of our trees, both coniferous and deciduous. On a clear day, like this last day in November, the silver and black symmetry of naked trunks pulsates with light as pure as that of a southwestern desert.

Our son Mark spent most of the summer of 1987 compiling a biological inventory of our property which he calls *Bioplum,* and he revised it in the spring of 1991. At that point, he had identified sixty-two native trees, nine naturalized trees, thirty-nine native shrubs, and eleven naturalized shrubs. He also discovered what we had long suspected: the center of biological diversity on our property is the hollow, especially along the stream bank, not only for trees and shrubs, but for wildflowers, birds, amphibians, reptiles, ferns, and mammals.

The ridgetop is basically composed of oaks and red maples, small American chestnuts, black gum, and mountain laurel, with here and there a single white pine or pitch pine. But in the hollow along the stream, large hemlocks dominate, and halfway down the road there is a fine grove of American beech trees. Rhododendron is the predominant understory species near the bottom of the mountain. Spicebush is the principal shrub near the top.

All that is evident at first glance. But when I look more closely I find many other species mixed in. I remember several years ago sitting on the hollow road bank waiting for Bruce to drive up. I was tucked back just beyond the entrance to the hollow, idly staring at the trees beside the stream, when one of them suddenly caught my attention. It was larger than the others, with a heavy black trunk that began forking several feet from the ground. Luckily the leaves were still on the tree because they tipped me off. They were long, thin, and light green—willow leaves, I decided. One black willow (*Salix nigra*) had migrated from the banks of the Little Juniata River to establish itself firmly in the deep muck of our bottomland. The predominant, flood-holding tree along the banks of the Ohio, Missouri, and Mississippi rivers, it is the largest of our willow species and ranges from New Brunswick to Georgia, and west as far as Oklahoma and Nebraska.

One of the most interesting of the trees that grows in the hollow is the cucumber magnolia (*Magnolia acuminata*), named for its distinctive fruit. Similar to a cucumber in its early stages, the fruits are two and a half to three inches long and are covered with red seeds set into the surface like grains of corn on the cob. It is especially acclimated to the mountain forests of the Carolinas and Tennessee where it grows sixty to ninety feet tall, but it

can be found as far north as western New York State. The
northernmost species of magnolia in America, it was
highly prized by plant collectors for shipping overseas to
English gardeners during colonial days. John Bartram of
Philadelphia, a botanist and collector, sent the first specimens to his patron Lord Petre in the middle of the eighteenth century.

Another plant collector, François Michaux, kept seeds
of the cucumber magnolia in fresh moss as he traveled
through the wilderness of western Pennsylvania in 1802.
On the banks of the Juniata River he discovered that "the
inhabitants of the remotest parts of Pennsylvania . . . pick
the cones when green, to infuse in whiskey, which gives it
a pleasant bitter."[8] Other than that, the seeds are palatable
to squirrels, mice, and some birds. Like the black willow,
the cucumber tree prefers moist soil. But it will grow on
rocky slopes as well and is also called mountain magnolia.

Tilia americana, American linden or basswood, is another common hollow tree. Its outstanding characteristic
is its flowers, beloved of honeybees which produce a de-
licious white honey from their nectar. According to the
naturalist Donald Culross Peattie, the scent from those
flowers is so piercing that even humans can smell it a mile
away. "The odor of the Lindens in bloom," he wrote,
"brings back to many of us the soaring wail of the tree-
toads, the first fireflies in the dusk, the banging of June
beetles on the window screens."[9] A large tree which flour-
ishes in low, wet woods, it grows in some places as high as
130 feet with a trunk three to four feet thick. Probably
what I notice most about it, though, are the shiny undersides of its heart-shaped leaves turned over on their stalks
by wind storms.

8. Peattie, *A Natural History of Trees,* pp. 276–77.
9. Ibid., p. 486.

Every time I walk up the hollow road, I am on the lookout for new species of trees and shrubs. A couple of weeks ago I made still another discovery. Just after crossing our wooden bridge at the fork with Margaret's old lane, I spotted red berries on a tall shrub growing near the stream. How had I (and Mark) missed this plant? With its bright fruits, it glowed conspicuously in the autumn light. Later I identified it as winterberry (*Ilex verticillata*), also called black alder because, like the true alders, it likes wet, swampy places. Its greenish or yellowish white, short-stalked blossoms, which bloom in late May or June, are inconspicuous, so it is easy to overlook the shrub then, but it frequently produces abundant fruits in autumn, drawing attention to itself. Those fruits often remain throughout the winter, like American bittersweet, and are sometimes gathered for use in winter bouquets. Ruffed grouse, cedar waxwings, and other fruit-eating, winter birds also relish its berries, but because I found only one shrub, I did not harvest any branches. Better to leave the berries to the birds in hopes that they will spread the seeds and produce more winterberry shrubs.

December

Any fool can destroy trees. They cannot run away; and if they could, they would still be destroyed—chased and hunted down as long as fun or a dollar could be got out of their bark hides, branching horns, or magnificent bole backbones.

—John Muir

DECEMBER 1. Gray December arrived on time to usher in the rains at last. A misty, moisty day heralded by a pair of Carolina wrens calling back and forth, one in the lilac bush beside the front porch, the other up on Sapsucker Ridge. So I put on my jacket and rubbers and took along an umbrella when I headed out for my usual morning walk.

The thick fog gave me insubstantial views of does fleeing across my path, but then, as I neared the Far Field, I glimpsed different movements in the mist ahead. Wild turkeys! I froze and strained to watch them feed as the fog isolated them and me. Since I could barely see them, I realized that they could not see me either. Slowly I eased my binoculars out of their case and watched eleven turkeys as they scratched up the fallen leaves like overgrown chickens and occasionally looked up. Shots in the valley did not disturb them, but a hammering in the distance sent them hurrying off into the woods. Nevertheless, watching turkeys undetected seemed a good omen to start the month.

DECEMBER 2. Another warm, overcast day with off and on rain. Perfect peace this first day of buck season—no skidders, no gunshots, no legions of men in orange stalking our trails and fields. Bruce and I went walking along our usual circuit in early afternoon, and the woods lay hushed and still. A four-point buck roused himself from where he had been lying, above the Far Field Road, and dashed across in front of us, heading down the mountain toward certain death, although we heard no shooting.

Off the Far Field Trail one of our hunter friends sat quietly, but he did tell us that neither he nor his young son had seen a buck all day. When we told him about the four-point, he was chagrined. He had decided to still-hunt instead of walking along the Far Field Road. Allowing a few select hunters to hunt responsibly on our property allowed us to continue to enjoy our land through the several weeks of deer season—buck, antlerless, and finally muzzle-loading—without fear of being shot by mistake, a privilege we have never had before. Yet, because of the overpopulation of deer which destroys the biodiversity of an area, and despite our own disinterest in hunting, we believe that we must allow man, now the only effective predator on deer, to "harvest" them.

There are other moral questions involved here. For many of the low- and middle-income people who live in our corner of Appalachia, hunting provides their only recreation and hunting season their only vacation. They don't constantly burn up oil and gas to go somewhere else. They are happy to live here and enjoy the outdoor privileges near at hand. In addition, we have seen little evidence of the trophy-hunting mentality of hunters from city and suburban areas. Our hunters, while happy to kill a buck with a big rack, are primarily meat-hunters; the venison from a couple of deer adds substantially to the family's food supply for the winter.

Then there is the question of health and the resources used to feed deer. If I had my choice in the matter, I would be happy to see deer and buffalo replace the cattle that overrun this country. Wild meat is almost fat free, highly nutritious, and has no harmful additives. If managed properly, those animals would live more harmoniously with the land than cattle do. For instance, the Pennsylvania Game Commission has been trying to persuade farmers to keep their cattle out of the streams. Even though the commission will supply free fencing for this program, very few farmers have agreed to cooperate. So thousands of miles of free-running streams that just happen to pass through a farmer's field are totally denuded of vegetation, their banks only trampled mud. This attitude, that the land is simply a commodity to exploit, is far more threatening to wildlife, and in fact to the entire ecosystem, than hunting. At least the Game Commission tries to arrive at equitable numbers of creatures that can be hunted, even on private property, without deleterious effects on the environment.

No such regulations are in effect for farmers and loggers—somehow we have convinced ourselves that their activities are benign. At the same time our government preaches the doctrine of sustainability to Third World countries. No wonder they resent our interference. A select segment of our population has always gotten rich from the exploitation of our natural resources, and the elite of Third World countries want the same privilege. The ordinary people, both here and in those countries, just want to live decently; "harvesting" surplus game animals provides needed protein for them and for us.

But I have no interest in killing any wild creature. They are far too interesting to observe when alive. And it was a source of joy to me today to see the does drifting out around the house near dusk as always, feeding calmly, as if their peaceful lives had not been disrupted.

DECEMBER 3. Tumultuous rains fell a good part of the night, those long-awaited rains of December, and for most of the day we had fog up to the driveway. Down in the hollow near dusk, Bruce and I found the stream flowing beautifully once again. For the first time in many months there were deep puddles in the road, and most of the side streams from the lumberman's land were also flowing.

The hollow was darkly overcast, lit only by the American beech trees which still retained their crop of dried, silvery beige leaves. They created peculiar points of light that seemed to shimmer and reflect what little illumination there was. The trunks of American beech trees, with their smooth, gray bark, have always reminded me of elephant skin, an allusion I thought was original to me. But today I was reading John Jerome's *Stone Work* and found that at least one other person has been similarly struck by the resemblance. "Beech bark looks like elephant skin," he writes, "a smooth gray membrane except where it turns corners and gets wrinkled and baggy" (p. 47). Such a discovery did not bother my sense of uniqueness. Instead, I welcomed a second beech-trunk admirer to the club, especially since I have recently learned that to a "good" forester, the American beech tree is a "trash" species which crowds out the "desirable" species.

This attitude, that there are "good" trees and "bad" trees, is already costing the lives of thousands of American women who die of ovarian cancer every year. The Pacific yew tree (*Taxus brevifolia*) was similarly treated as a "bad" tree by the timber industry and was extirpated as old-growth forests were cut and replanted with commercially "good" trees, primarily Douglas fir. Loggers even used Pacific yew to break the fall of Douglas fir trees to prevent that "valuable" wood from splintering. Valuable to whom? Certainly not to cancer victims. Once researchers discovered that the bark and needles of Pacific yew contained the powerful anticancer compound taxol, they also discovered that it took the death of six 100-year-old-trees to get enough taxol to treat one patient. By then, there were not enough mature Pacific yew trees in the world left to provide the amount of taxol they needed. And scientists have not yet been able to synthesize taxol in their laboratories. Until there is a major breakthrough, which may never happen and certainly will not happen in time to help most cancer victims now, doctors must depend on the "natural" product, the Pacific yew tree that not only grows half as fast as other conifers, but also grows only in the secluded shade of old-growth forests.

With such graphic proof that, in fact, we still do not know the possible uses of most plants and trees, I would think that foresters and other "managers" might be humbled in the face of nature's bounty. But apparently not, since their remedy for "bad" beech trees is to kill beech sprouts with herbicides, so that other, more desirable species will grow. This approach is particularly distressing because already beech trees are falling victim to beech bark disease, caused by a beech scale insect that attacks the bark and wounds it. Then a fungus enters the wood and kills the tree. So far, the disease has not reached our hollow, but it will inevitably come.

I cannot imagine our woods without the American beech tree (*Fagus grandifolia*). Once again Donald Culross Peattie had it right when he wrote, "A Beech is, in almost any landscape where it appears, the finest tree to be seen . . . As the sun of Indian summer bathes the great tree, it stands in a profound autumnal calm, enveloped in a golden light that hallows all about it." Peattie admits that the wood is tough to split and knotty, yet decays easily, and that it has little commercial use. But he sums up my feelings when he concludes, "Let other trees do the work of the world. Let the Beech stand, where still it holds its ground, a monument to past glories."[1] And to present beauty, I might add.

DECEMBER 4. Today I wandered through the woods and fields, searching for evidence of life in the remnants that have been left behind by hibernating insects, migrating birds, and dormant weeds.

The center of the Far Field was especially lovely because it has been taken over recently by a new weed—bristlegrass or foxtail. To an artist, its golden beige color is striking against the darker grays and browns of other dried weeds, but to farmers it is a scourge that chokes out more valuable crops. Wildlife champions can also defend bristlegrass because its seeds provide valuable food for wintering songbirds and wild turkeys. Every time I visit the Far Field, flocks of dark-eyed juncos and American tree sparrows erupt from the ground at the base of the weeds where they have been feeding.

Four black locust saplings grow in the midst of the bristlegrass. Several days ago I discovered a perfect paper wasp nest hanging from the end of a tree branch and swinging in the breeze like a Chinese paper lantern. Today I found its tattered remains strewn on the ground.

I picked up a portion of it and examined it more closely. Its layers of gray, light-weight paper enclosed the hexagonal cells like envelopes. The cells were empty, though,

1. Peattie, *A Natural History of Trees*, pp. 179–80, 182.

because its former inhabitants had left the nest and died at the end of the summer. Only the new queen lived on, fertilized by the males and now hibernating for the winter in the cracks of an old log, perhaps, or the crevices of an attic or barn. But in her minute sperm sac she had stored away the beginnings of next year's colony.

When spring comes, she will arouse from a deathlike torpor and start to construct a new nest. Then she will lay the first eggs and tend the larvae until they hatch into workers. They will take over most of her tasks—enlarging the nest, keeping it cool by fanning, bringing in water, and feeding the larvae—and from then on she will be an egg-laying machine.

Back in the eighteenth century, western European scientists watched members of the Vespid wasp family construct their nests. Previously, paper had been made from rags, but it was these female worker wasps that demonstrated how wood pulp could be turned into paper. A wasp would land on an old board or dried weed and, walking backward, would rasp off a long strip with her mandibles and roll it into a ball beneath her thorax. The ball was then carried in her mouth back to the nest where it was well macerated with fluid regurgitated from her crop. The resultant mass was then tamped smoothly to the end of the nest by her mandibles.

In addition to teaching Western man how to make paper from wood, wasps have also been important because of the many insects they prey on. Although wasps and their larvae do eat nectar, like honeybees, they obtain their protein from dead and dying material and insects. By the end of the season, it has been estimated that every day the workers bring three to four thousand prey loads of insect larvae, spiders, and flies to the nest.

We label such wasps as pests—yellow jackets and hornets, we call them—yet they are valuable creatures in our ecosystem. They sting only to defend their nests which, near the end of the summer, are at the height of their production. Eventually the queen stops laying and the nest is deserted. The males go off in pursuit of future queens they can fertilize. Then they die, leaving a whole new generation of queens to winter over and begin new colonies the following spring.

DECEMBER 5. It was over almost before it had begun, that icing-on-the-cake snow that fell lightly for several hours and then petered out. But there was enough snow to dust the earth with white and change the entire complexion of the season from autumn to winter, at least for the day—a gentle reminder of what is to come.

The snow had all of the beauty, but none of the hassles, of most snowstorms, clinging to branches and weeds and covering the lawn and trails with a thin white blanket, yet not imperiling our access up the road by piling up and drifting.

Despite the lustrous, pearly gray skies, there was plenty of color—the rosy brown of the bowed grasses with their patina of white, the bright green of evergreen hemlock trees, rhododendron and laurel leaves bowed down and patched with white. Dark-eyed juncos flashed their white-lined tails, white-throated sparrows "zipped" from the thickets, and white-breasted nuthatches "yank-yanked" up and down tree trunks. The punctuated calls of downy woodpeckers, the shrieks of a flock of blue jays, and the loud yelps of a pileated woodpecker were a noisy contrast to the one American crow that flapped silently over the whitened field.

Along the Short Circuit Trail a huge, hollow black oak tree had snapped off about fifteen feet up its trunk and blocked the way with massive limbs spattered in every direction. When had it fallen, I wondered, and who had heard it crash? Club moss had been crushed beneath the debris, its yellow candles broken and askew.

Then I stopped to gaze down the powerline right-of-way at a large doe that was gazing back at me. She thought she was invisible with her brown coat turning gray, but against the snow she stood out, the single sign of mammal life I saw that morning, her tracks the only ones, except for mine, that marred the white blanket.

In the valley the snow had barely patched the surface, and it remained mostly brown and green. The snow line clearly ran about halfway up the ridge. So there I was, enjoying the muffled peace of the first snow, while below me life went on as usual. What a difference only a few hundred feet in elevation can make.

DECEMBER 6. Most of the snow had melted by today, so I went out to search for the inconspicuous green plants that are usually hidden by heavy undergrowth in the summer and snow and ice in the winter.

Two of my favorite evergreen plants—partridgeberry and teaberry—produce red fruits. This combination of red and green is especially appropriate in December when those Christmas colors festoon many homes. Teaberry (*Gaultheria procumbens*) usually has one berry hanging beneath the waxy leaves of each plant. Since these berries, as well as the leaves, are edible and have a distinct, wintergreen flavor, I was pleased to discover that most plants support from two to five berries this year. They will spice up my winter walks and will also provide food for ruffed grouse, wild turkeys, and white-tailed deer.

The fruit of partridgeberry (*Mitchella repens*) is classified as barely edible for humans but ruffed grouse, wild turkeys, red foxes, striped skunks, along with common bobwhites, eat it, hence its popular name. Another name, "twinberry," refers to the way its paired white flowers merge at the base like Siamese twins, producing one red fruit. This trailing ground cover also has paired green leaves with light midveins and is usually found in moist woodlands, particularly beneath white pine trees.

Club mosses are other evergreen ground covers especially noticeable at this time of year. Closely allied to ferns, they are herbaceous plants with small leaves and a single unbranched stem. Like ferns, they also reproduce by spores and were the first land plants to develop roots, stems, and leaves. Two hundred and fifty million years ago they grew one hundred feet tall; now they are reduced to, at most, a foot in height.

They are commonly called "ground pines" because of their resemblance to evergreen trees. Of the nearly two dozen species of club mosses in North America, I have discovered five on the mountain. The first, running pine (*Lycopodium complanatum*), grows in thick profusion beneath a huge hemlock tree in the hollow. This attractive, creeping club moss is also called "Christmas green" since it is often used in making wreaths.

Shining club moss (*Lycopodium lucidulum*), a lucid green, upright, and bristly plant, grows under a white pine tree, also in the hollow. It is especially easy to identify because of the orange yellow, kidney-shaped spore cases found at the base of its upper leaves.

Several years ago Bruce and I discovered a few examples of ground cedar (*Lycopodium tristachyum*), a blue green club moss that looks like a tiny evergreen tree growing in a fan shape and so is nicknamed "ground pine." Wolf's claw or staghorn club moss (*Lycopodium clavatum*) sprawls across the top of First Field Trail. Its upright, branching stems look like deer horns or wolf claws, according to the imaginative taxonomists who first named this plant. Because its evergreen trailing branches were once widely used for Christmas decorations, it is the least common of the club moss species.

The most common club moss on our mountain is the

tree club moss (*Lycopodium obscurum*), which resembles a thickly branched, miniature pine tree. At this time of year it still has its yellow, cylindrical, conelike strobili growing from its top like candelabras. When I touch them, a powder of yellow spores fills the air, reminding me of their use in fireworks and as "flash powder" for old cameras because they catch fire quickly and cause a small explosive flash.

Tree club mosses are supposed to be found in damp, open woods and along the edges of forest bogs, yet they grow by the hundreds on the dry, open, powerline right-of-way as well as in the leaf duff beneath hardwood trees, the needle duff of white pines, and even among the dried grasses at the Far Field and the top of First Field. I also find them in more traditional areas, in wet depressions at the top of Sapsucker Ridge, in a small wetland at the base of First Field Trail, and in the shaded, evergreen areas of the hollow.

The club mosses, teaberries and partridgeberries, along with the evergreen woodland ferns, Christmas ferns, and a wide variety of mosses and lichens, make walking in the woods a greener experience than one would expect in December.

DECEMBER 7. Autumn has returned again—forty-nine degrees with bright sunshine. But by the time I took a walk in mid-afternoon only a broad band of golden light low on the horizon lit up the silvery gray, overcast sky. Although I startled a few deer along the way, the woods was mostly silent. Near dusk we had another Pinatubo sunset of deep rose spreading across the western sky, lighting the earth as well as the heavens.

In contrast to my paucity of day sightings, Steve, by being out at night, has had two enviable experiences. One occurred as he walked up the road after midnight and heard loud thrashing noises coming up behind him. He sat down quietly, expecting to see a deer. Instead, a black bear walked within ten feet of him and then turned and went down to the stream to drink. Steve whistled and moved about, but the bear never did notice him.

Last night he went down to lift weights in the barn at 9:30 P.M., and when he put on the barnyard light he spotted a gray phase eastern screech owl sitting on a beam under the barn overhang. It blinked a few times in the bright light and flew off.

I may not go out much at night but I do spend time in our cellar which, it turns out, has a surprising amount of wildlife in it for late autumn: hibernating woolly bear caterpillars curled up in corners, assorted species of spiders, and even one young eastern milk snake (*Lampropeltis triangulum*). I first spotted it back in early October next to the bottom step, curled up, its head turning and its questing tongue darting in and out. Since milk snakes hatch from eggs in August and September and since they are nine inches long at that time, I assumed it was a young snake. It was beautifully colored with the brownish red splotches on a grayish white background characteristic of milk snakes.

For weeks I had to be careful when I went down to the basement to do the laundry since I often found the snake coiled up directly on my path to the washing machine. I always detoured carefully around it, saying a friendly "hello" and wondering to myself how it found enough to eat. Surely such a small creature would be incapable of killing and eating rodents, which are the principal food of milk snakes. Possibly, though, it had eaten its siblings when they had first hatched. As Roger Conant and Joseph T. Collins warn in their field guide *Reptiles and Amphibians, Eastern/Central North America,* the genus *Lampropeltis,* to which milk snakes belong, are powerful constrictors. They are well known for killing and eating other serpents, including venomous ones. For this reason, they should not be kept with smaller reptiles, even those of their own species.

Why should I tolerate a milk snake in the basement? An old Italian saying holds that a milk snake in the basement brings good luck, and we could certainly use that. But I think that "good luck," in this case, means "no rodents." To many country dwellers that would be luck enough since rodents and old farmhouses appear to go hand-in-hand. I suspect, however, that most people would have a difficult time choosing between rodents or snakes in their cellars.

Yet our milk snake will do me no harm, hibernating, in all probability, somewhere among the detritus of the cellar storage area. Next to garter snakes, milk snakes are the most common snakes in Pennsylvania. Unfortunately, they do have a coloration pattern similar to northern copperheads and are often killed because of this. They were also accused of milking cows, a totally erroneous belief, probably because they were frequently found in cow barns searching for rodents. Another name for them is "house snake" since they do frequent human dwellings. They kill three to four times more mice in a year than a hawk or owl, and considering our recent change of heart toward birds of prey, it might be prudent to be at least as charitable where snakes are concerned.

Snakes, though, continue to get bad press that they don't deserve, especially in a temperate climate like Pennsylvania's where most snakes are harmless. Even the few poisonous species, timber rattlesnakes and northern copperheads, are rare now, and the endangered Massasauga rattlesnake is downright shy. The only snakes that occasionally fall out of trees and startle people are harmless black rat and black racer snakes, but even they do not lurk, waiting to leap onto unsuspecting bystanders.

So, when our milk snake emerges from hibernation next spring, I will continue to step carefully around it because I have made my decision. I do prefer snakes to rodents in my basement. Such a colorful, useful, and interesting creature should be encouraged, not feared.

DECEMBER 8. Forty-seven degrees and mostly overcast with a rustling breeze and the smell of spring in the air. It was time to hang out a load of wash to the sound of three calling eastern bluebirds investigating the nest box. A northern flicker also called, and, of course, the merry Carolina wren. All traces of snow were gone as imminent winter again retreated before the balmy late fall tones of beige and brown, silver and gold, gray and white, and every imaginable shade in between.

So this is what a southern winter is like, I told myself as I sat outside on a lawn chair listening to the "weet-su, weet-su, weet-su" of Carolina wrens rejoicing in life no matter the season or whether or not it is mating time. First I heard two, then three Carolina wrens competing back and forth, sounding like echoes of one another, one down in the front yard, two on Sapsucker Ridge—an Indian summer chorus of joy. All the birds were confused by the weather. Black-capped chickadees sang "fee-be," which made me think that for some birds, at least, it is warmth and not increasing daylight that triggers their song mechanism.

On Laurel Ridge Trail in mid-afternoon I heard the downscale, explosive whistle of a red-tailed hawk and watched it soaring near treetop height, catching the winds off Laurel Ridge. I lay down on the Far Field Road bank, wrapped mostly in utter silence which was punctuated once by a scolding gray squirrel and twice by a calling hairy woodpecker. But as I walked on along the edge of the Far Field, first a wild turkey flapped off and then a herd of doe fled. I kept blinking my eyes at the dull, reflective December sheen lying over the sunless landscape, almost as if I was snowblind. The dark was rising despite the warmth.

Lastly, I sat in a sea of dried grasses at the top of First Field, watching the light drain from the earth. The straw-colored grasses were heavy with seed heads swishing in the breeze which lightened up the bland gray background of sky and woods.

Raining by dusk.

DECEMBER 9. An amazing fifty-six degrees at dawn, overcast, dark, with a spit of rain in the air. The mist brought the deer out from hiding, including five does and a six-point buck. The latter excited the interest of one doe who sniffed his legs, his belly, and even his muzzle as they grazed head to head. She sparred once with him, but he wandered away as she looked after him. Both then fed separately in the flat area, pulling up mouthfuls of grass. Distant gunfire sent him up into the woods and security of Laurel Ridge. The doe watched him out of sight and finally resumed her eating.

By 10:30 in the morning a little weak sunshine appeared and the sky began to brighten, so I walked down the road. Just after passing the remains of our old corral, I noticed pieces of bark raining down. I looked up into a large tree to the right of the road and spotted a raccoon about fifty feet above me. It saw me at the same time, turned around on the branch and hissed.

I tried to respond reassuringly by saying quietly, "I won't hurt you." But I achieved the opposite effect. Trying to get down the tree as fast as it could, it more or less tumbled earthward from branch to branch. When it ran out of branches, it scrambled down the tree trunk, spread-eagling at one point in what looked like a desperate attempt to hold on. Finally, it regained its balance and plunged head first down the trunk, free-falling the last fifteen feet to the ground below and rolling over. Then, almost as if it had already forgotten its fright, it sat up on its haunches and tried to clean itself off. It was a big, portly raccoon, a rounded-off teddy bear of a creature, and I wondered about its short-term memory.

Even as I stood on the road watching, it waddled nonchalantly across the road and down into the stream. First it drank deeply. Then it climbed back on the bank and sitting down on its back haunches again, it proceeded to thoroughly lick clean its belly and back legs for several minutes. It seemed to have forgotten my existence because it then waddled slowly up the streambed, stopping to clean itself a couple more times while I followed along the road slightly above and behind it.

Frequently it paused to sniff the air, and I stopped too, so perhaps it did not see me even though I was in plain view. It trundled up through the dried weeds of the guesthouse bank below the pear tree, sniffed along the foundations underneath the bedroom, and finally moved around to the front of the house. First it tried to get under the front porch by squeezing past a downspout and a swinging wire, falling on its back like a clown each time the wire smacked it. I began to think the raccoon was a comedian of little brain until it squeezed under the lattice work protecting the furnace beneath the guesthouse front porch. Apparently it is spending the winter there.

Later, after hearing Steve's account of the noises coming from under the house, I decided that the raccoon was a "she," and that she was communally "nesting" for the winter under the guesthouse. Although not true hibernators, like bears, raccoons build up a heavy layer of fat and come out to forage only on warm winter days. That raccoon was so fat it moved like an obese person, swaying clumsily, its large rear end elevated high above its spindly back legs.

DECEMBER 10. Thirty-six degrees and clearing at dawn after rain in the early morning hours. A common raven flew over the house "cronking." The First Field wood frog pond was full and the stream was back to its usual depth, ending the drought here on our mountain.

Up in the corner of First Field, lit and warmed by the morning sun, it was woodpecker land. Several pileateds as well as a hairy and a red-bellied worked over the trees. A flock of eight tufted titmice flew in to forage and scold me as I sat quietly at the woods' edge. Black-capped chickadees and white-breasted nuthatches also appeared, followed by calling Carolina wrens. Next I heard the "tut-tutting" of American robins.

"Pishing" at the First Field thicket brought out a bevy of birds including a northern flicker. Walking slowly on, watching, listening, occasionally "pishing," I saw a downy woodpecker as well as a flock of dark-eyed juncos, American tree sparrows, and house finches, another hairy woodpecker, and a female northern cardinal. Later, I listened to the cawing of American crows as I sat in the Sapsucker Ridge woods near a moldering old tree. The tree was broken off about fifteen feet up and its inner bark, looking like crumbled soil, had fallen in large chunks to the ground. Even while I sat there, another chunk fell to the ground. I was watching soil in the making.

Walking back along the Far Field Road, a high-pitched "zee" alerted me to a brown creeper skittering up tree trunks like a high-strung brown mouse. With its bark-colored back and white breast, it blends almost perfectly with the tree bark it probes in search of insects. No other bird looks or acts like it. Further identifying marks include a thin, down-curving beak and the habit of spiraling up tree trunks. Here on our mountain, it keeps company with golden-crowned kinglets, so I cannot identify it solely by its high-pitched "zee" which sounds similar to the calling of the kinglets. Lately, it seems as if our mountain hosts a larger and larger population of brown creepers every fall and winter, and often I can sit quite close to them and watch them at work since they are almost as bold as golden-crowned kinglets.

From the top of First Field, I gazed down at the view of field and woods and distant hilltops. But even as I admired the beauty, I was struck by how little a person can interact with a view, other than to admire it. To experience nature, one must get down into the view and explore the woods, the fields, the thickets, the hillsides for what is there. Our "view-oriented" society prefers to gaze from afar—from cars, from lookouts, from airplanes—rather than to get into the picture and participate. No doubt such an attitude is a legacy of our television-viewing culture, where many people are convinced that seeing it on television is as good as being there, and, in most cases, even better since the camera can focus in on the minutiae or edit out the slow parts when not much happens.

I walked down First Field Trail into the view and sat on a log writing notes. Suddenly a fox squirrel with a bobbed tail trotted past, intent on searching the ground for nuts. Either it had had a close encounter with a predator or it had been born with half a tail. By walking into the view I was rewarded with a new observation—new to me at least. Whether my experience was unique was not important. What mattered was that I saw something for myself. It had not been staged, edited, or improved for my viewing pleasure.

Other doses of reality were not as pleasant. First, I found two enormous clots of dried blood about a quarter of a mile above where I had discovered a dead six-point buck the other day. Evidently it had been badly wounded and then had struggled on to die near the old farm dump. During an afternoon walk in the hollow I found a four-point buck lying dead near the stream. He had a large gunshot hole through the upper part of his back, and his eyes were open and still intact, unlike the six-point whose eyes had already been gouged out by scavengers, probably American crows. The four-point also had his mouth kindly closed in contrast to the six-point which had his tongue exposed. The four-point looked peaceful in death, but his haunches, like the six-point's, had already been partially eaten.

Finally, I ended this day sitting up above the old farm dump area near sunset, watching several gray squirrels gathering food, leaping from treetop to treetop, graceful beyond reason, just as such a day as this was a day of grace filled with sunlight and peace—and reality.

DECEMBER II. After two postponements, the local magistrate finally held a hearing regarding the breaking of our gate lock by the lumberman's son back on October 1, the first day of their lumbering operation. Bruce and I arrived early to find the small waiting room overflowing with his supporters and relatives, including the lumberman himself and his lawyer, all of whom studiously avoided us. We, with our pitiful complaint, were an embarrassment to them. Bruce was able to read the newspaper while we waited, but I was captive to their conversation, which seemed directed at us. As I listened, I felt as if the same conversation was being repeated that I had heard nearly two years ago in our lawyer's office when we had reached, we thought, an agreement to trade trees and protect the hollow.

The lawyer started off by commenting that he had to "serve his country" over the weekend by attending his National Guard unit in Pittsburgh. The lumberman replied by citing the exemplary qualities of a forester who had formerly worked for him, but who now was "high up in the National Guard in Pittsburgh." It *was* the same conversation.

From there, they improvised. The lumberman, it seems, has a vacation cabin in West Virginia among the "hillbillies," as he pejoratively referred to them. I assume they also hunt there since they had previously asked the lawyer if he had "gotten his buck yet," standard bonding talk among males in this area at this time. But the lumberman chose to talk about the outdoor "salad bar" they provide for the deer, as if to demonstrate what animal lovers they are.

Finally, the state trooper emerged from a previous hearing, and we greeted him cheerfully, carrying on our own small talk with him until we were all called into what was a small courtroom with three rows of benches. The magistrate, tall and distinguished looking with silver hair and a mustache, appeared from a side door near the front garbed in a long black robe. The pleasant, round-faced trooper sat at one table, and across from him sat the accused and his lawyer. Bruce and I sat in the front row of the benches. The lumberman sat with a lady whom I took to be his daughter-in-law and two men I didn't know in the back corner of the third row as far from us as possible.

First the trooper told his story, followed by Bruce telling his. Then, the lumberman's lawyer, playing his role as "trial attorney" to the hilt, questioned the trooper.

"Where did you encounter the accused and Mr. Bonta? Did you talk to the accused and ask him why he broke the lock?" And so on. It was quickly obvious he was trying to demonstrate that the lumberman had the right to use the road and so had broken the lock. Grandstanding to the au-

dience with extravagant gestures and hyperbole, the lawyer patently ignored Bruce and called on the accused to
testify, repeating again the point that he had a legitimate
right to drive up the road since he had equipment on the
mountain to timber his father's property. He kept trying
to make a court trial out of what was to be only a hearing,
bringing up as many irrelevant facts as he could to cloud
the issue of whether or not the accused had committed an
illegal act by breaking our lock.

As he droned on and on, Bruce finally asked the magistrate, "Since we were told by our lawyer that his services
were not necessary for a hearing, can I assume that these
accusations and innuendos by their lawyer are irrelevant?"

The magistrate spoke, cutting incisively through the
lawyer's smokescreen by saying that the issue at this hearing was simply, "Did the accused willfully break the lock?"
Since he did, he was guilty. He fined the accused $100.00
for criminal mischief and $65.00 for court costs. But be-
cause Bruce had failed to mention that he wanted reim-
bursement for the new lock, their lawyer pointed out, we
were not entitled to it. The magistrate agreed.

The lumberman burst out loudly in the back, "All that
fuss for an $18.00 lock," making it clear that he had no
fundamental understanding of right or wrong in this issue; he wants everything to go his way without acknowl-
edging our concerns or rights or attempting to deal fairly
with us. We felt no elation over our victory, and our faces
reflected our somber thoughts.

Afterward, the lawyer gathered his flock together outside, and we heard, as we passed their smoldering faces,
"Let me tell you what we can do." About what, we wondered? Our lawyer had been trying to get their lawyer to at
least suggest the possibility of selling the land to us now,
before they strip it to the road, but we doubted that their
lawyer would make any attempt to discuss *that* issue with

them. In the last year, all he had done was stonewall our lawyer whenever he asked him whether he could bring us together with his client—about the logging, the road, buying the property, in fact, every initiative we had tried, hoping to solve our differences without resorting to the expense of going to court.

In contrast to the lumberman and his cohorts, all of whom were clothed to the nines in respectability, I was dressed for the hearing in my hiking best so I could walk back up the hollow road afterward, allowing Bruce to drive on to his office. I was rewarded near the big pulloff with a close look at several foraging golden-crowned kinglets in the hemlocks plus a large dark-eyed junco flock. As usual, the former flew close and gave me a wonderful view, while the latter kept their distance. At the height of their activity, I suddenly spotted a red-tailed hawk looming overhead, but it quickly flew off when it saw me. Up above the first pulloff, a winter wren called from the stream bank. Just beyond the forks, a large flock of house finches were feeding on tulip poplar seeds.

DECEMBER 12. The days of grace are over. Bruce called the lumberman this morning to try for a last minute settlement, but he was adamant that he will cut everything down to the road. And he will sue us in court for road access up the hollow. I listened on the other phone and again tried to decide, "What is truth?"

Bruce asked him why he was reneging on his agreement to trade trees with us. He reminded the lumberman that, as we had agreed at the meeting in our lawyer's office, their forester had finished marking the traded trees and had shown them to Bruce over a year ago. Bruce had then asked him for his calculations so we could call in our own expert to verify them, but the forester had said he would have to talk to the lumberman about that before sharing his figures. We had never heard another word. But now, on the telephone, the lumberman was denying that his forester had ever marked the trees or had ever met with Bruce. And over and over he kept saying, "You drove me to cut all the trees." The more I listened, the more I felt as if we were caught in a tissue of deception. What were their intentions—the lumberman, the forester, the lawyer, and the supporting cast of loggers and relatives?

One thing was clear though. The lumberman would not sell us the land at any price. And he would not stay 200 feet above the road. "Those trees have to be cut," he kept repeating like a mantra.

So after listening to a forty-five-minute harangue, most of which bore little or no resemblance to what had actually happened over the last six years, Bruce gave up. Peace-making was not an option nor was compromise. He called our lawyer and asked him to go ahead and file the motion he had prepared requesting a court injunction to keep them 200 feet above the road. Unfortunately, because hunting season ends in a few days, we had to settle for the earliest date possible—December 19—and the worst possible time. If only we had not tried for a peaceful settlement; if only we had allowed our lawyer to go ahead weeks ago when he first learned that they intended to cut down to the road. But no, we have remained innocents until the end, still unable to believe that what a man, especially one who devoutly attends church twice a week, says is not necessarily what he will do. Our lawyer, more experienced in dealing with humanity's weaknesses, has all along seen the truth of the matter. But we, peace-lovers that we are, continued to hope. When he first urged us to file a court injunction, our lawyer had felt hopeful. But as soon as he learned the time of the hearing—8:00 A.M.— he seemed to lose heart.

"That judge will never allow expert testimony in the time we have," he told us. But expert testimony was what we were banking on, testimony from our retired U.S. Forest Service friend on the lumberman's logging practices and from the professor of geology at Penn State who had studied the instability of our hollow for years. But Bruce remained confident in our legal system, in its concern with the common citizen's safety. After all, hadn't the magistrate protected our rights?

On the other hand, he was leaving nothing to chance. So he headed down to the courthouse to study old deeds. He also dropped in at the Soil Conservation office and asked the two women employees if he could see a copy of the Soil Erosion Control Plan the lumberman had filed with them. The more he read, the angrier he became. The two women had inspected the site back in October with the lumberman's son, and they explained what they had seen and what had been promised: the number of skid roads, the amount of land that would be cut, the soil erosion control measures they were taking, such as temporary culverts at all stream crossings. "He seemed earnestly concerned to do the job right," one of the women said.

Bruce told them that since they had visited, the tempo of road-building and cutting had been significantly increased. They insisted that they had not been told that the lumberman was going to cut down to the road. Although they were warmly sympathetic and wished Bruce well in court, they could do nothing to help. Our lumberman, in fact, enjoyed a good reputation with them because he always filed a Soil Erosion Control Plan before logging an area. They did, however, give Bruce a copy of the plan.

While Bruce was involved in the nitty-gritty, I was out enjoying my last reprieve, watching a male downy woodpecker close up as he examined a dead snag down in the hollow above the road. He moved fast—up, down, and around the snag, sometimes retracing his path, stabbing here and there with his bill. Otherwise, the woods were hushed and seemingly deserted, once again waiting for a change.

DECEMBER 13. Today I added a new creature to my basement list: a live salamander in the toilet! Needless to say, I was amazed. Grabbing a jar, I scooped it out of the toilet bowl and took it up to the kitchen table where I examined it.

Let it be known that I am a salamander lover. Picking up a wriggling, slippery salamander and looking it straight in the eyes is one of my pleasures in life. This salamander lay still as soon as I put it on the table next to a ruler. It was four and three-quarter inches long with a uniformly dark back and a gray underside. Through my hand lens I could see a faint sprinkling of minuscule white spots. With that data recorded, I thought I would be able to identify it, so, in the pouring rain, I took the salamander down to the springhouse where I released it.

Then the real work began—putting a name to the nondescript creature. For an hour I pored over Conant and Collins's *Reptiles and Amphibians* and slowly narrowed the possibilities down to four species—the ravine, the Wehrle's, the valley and ridge, and the lead-backed type of the red-backed salamander. All are members of the *Plethodon* or lungless salamander family: they have neither gills nor lungs but breathe through their skins and the lining of their mouths. For this reason they must live in damp places.

According to Maurice Brooks in *The Appalachians,* "unglaciated Appalachia is the salamander hunter's paradise" (p. 256). Furthermore, it is believed that the Family *Plethodontidae* originated in the Appalachians, possibly the only major vertebrate group that has done so, because there are more species and races and greater populations of salamanders here than in any other part of the world. And our hollow has always been rich in both numbers and species; it is ideal habitat for woodland salamanders. A recent study of logging operations in New York State found that many reptiles and salamanders were crushed by bulldozers and skidders, especially when the woods were wet, because the creatures stayed either on or just below the ground surface, so I wonder how many will be left in the hollow after the logging is finished?

Wehrle's, ravine, valley and ridge, and red-backed salamanders all belong to the woodland salamander group which is abundant in wooded eastern North America. They are abroad only at night or during heavy rains and eat earthworms and insects. This group has no aquatic larval stage, so their small clusters of eggs laid in damp places hatch out into fully formed salamanders.

After much comparing of descriptions and studying of illustrations, I decided that the toilet bowl salamander may have been a Wehrle's salamander (*Plethodon wehrlei*). That would be appropriate because this salamander was named for R. W. Wehrle, a naturalist from Indiana, Pennsylvania, who first collected a specimen of it. Or it could have been the recently discovered and named valley and ridge salamander (*Plethodon hoffmani*). That would also be appropriate because it is chiefly found in the Valley-and-Ridge Province of west central Pennsylvania where we live, down through West Virginia and Virginia. But I could not be 100 percent certain of its identity because salamanders vary so widely in coloration from one area to another. However, both the Wehrle's and the valley and ridge's habitat—upland forest—seemed right. So did their length—4 to 5 ¼ inches for the Wehrle's and 3 ⁹⁄₁₆ to 5 ⅜ for the valley and ridge. While the Wehrle's coloration is dark and plain-backed in the northern part of its range, with a gray belly, a white throat, and some white spotting, the valley and ridge is dark-backed with a white mottled, mostly dark belly and a white throat. But my specimen did not have a white throat, a characteristic of both salamanders.

Who knows? It may have been a new species. As Brooks says, Appalachia is "a happy land where even today new species and races turn up with surprising frequency" (p. 256). Is it possible I discovered a new woodland salamander, *Plethodon toiletei?*

DECEMBER 14. Raining and warm in the morning. But in mid-afternoon a sea change occurred—fierce winds and plunging temperatures. By nightfall it was twenty-four degrees with a howling gale which shook the house so hard that it shuddered.

Bruce and I spent the afternoon in the hollow photographing the slopes and the log end that had already tumbled down the mountainside, across the road, and into the stream during the logging 200 feet above the road. We were hoping to show the photos to the judge as evidence of the "clear and present danger" to us of lumbering so close to the road on such steep slopes.

It was while we were doing this that the weather changed from a warmish, driving rain to sleet and snow. But Bruce doggedly persisted, clambering up and down the slippery slopes, hauling his heavy camera and tripod, while I posed in the stream with the log end or drove the car on up the hollow for more photos. But I could not fight the dread feeling I had of fruitlessly trying to oppose the right of a landowner to plunder his land with no regard for those who are metaphorically "downwind."

In addition to that depressing work, I also checked out the condition of the dead four-point buck. To my surprise, it had been dragged several yards to the bottom of the road bank and its back and side covered with a log, two large pieces of bark, and dead leaves. Only its head and rear end, much of which had been consumed, remained exposed. Probably the work of a black bear, we finally concluded. But just in case, Bruce took photos so we could show them to wildlife experts for their opinion.

DECEMBER 15. The winds brought down trees all over the area. A huge maple had fallen below the forks, which Bruce cleared before breakfast. Our forester friend, who was to come this morning to look over the "responsible" logging operation and give us his opinion, called last evening to postpone his visit. A large tree had come down on his property, bringing a nest of wires along with it.

By the time I ventured out late in the morning after the wind had died, the sky was blue to the horizon, and I hoped for a "sign" to lighten my heavy heart. Already I mourned the total destruction of the hollow. Horrors of a far worse nature are perpetrated daily worldwide; the strong triumph over the weak, creating an endless tragedy of hatred and suffering, of lies and deceptions. Despots, large and small, crush the powerless underfoot, aided by machines, by armies, by police.

That is why I love the natural world so much. Nature is clean, egoless, lacking hatreds and jealousies. Death occurs at every level, but only so that all can eat. No creature gets more than it needs; none accumulates wealth to the detriment of others. Yet there seems to be a measure of care and regard in some species for others of their kind, the sort of dawning of understanding, morality, call it what you will, that launched humanity on its way.

Humanity has taken a wrong turning and pays little heed to the peacemakers, prophets, and other visionaries who try to call out a warning. "Give me a sign," I pleaded as I walked along. But only the wind and creaking trees filled the empty silence.

DECEMBER 16. Seventeen degrees with a howling wind that calmed down as the day progressed. It was the first day of doe season and I heard a few shots, so I waited until early afternoon to go walking. I found a pile of deer guts to the left of the Far Field Trail and followed a trail of blood to a log at the edge of First Field. As I descended the top of First Field, two large does jumped up from the weeds. One ran while the other stood and looked at me even after I said, "If I were a hunter, you'd be dead." Finally it ran off.

When is a hunter not a hunter? When he or she is a "hunter-in-naturalist." According to Edward O. Wilson, in his lyrical book *Biophilia,* "the naturalist is a civilized hunter. He goes alone into a field or woodland and closes his mind to everything but that time and place, so that life around him presses in on all the senses and small details grow in significance. . . . The hunter-in-naturalist knows that he does not know what is going to happen" (p. 103).

Wilson is a world authority on tropical ant species and spends most of his naturalist time in rainforests where the variety of life forms and numbers of still undiscovered species is enormous. He is liable to make a unique observation whenever he goes walking, but even in the woods of Pennsylvania, curious things can happen. So I have the same feeling of expectation that Wilson describes every time I go walking. Although my discoveries will probably not be new to science, they will be new to me. And such experiences are what make my life a continual joy. I am, in other words, a victim of "biophilia," what Wilson defines as an "innate tendency to focus on life and lifelike processes" (p. 1). Wilson is convinced that all humanity has this tendency because of our biological inheritance.

Cities and civilization—so recent to humanity's experience—are unnatural. People need greenery and contact with wild creatures to be mentally healthy. Wilson also believes that the more we learn about nature, the more we will respect it. Certainly I have found myself continually amazed by discoveries biologists are making about the intricate lives of the lowliest creatures. I can empathize with people, like the late naturalist-writer Edwin Way Teale, who refused to kill even a fly in his home because flies are such interesting creatures. Instead he would catch them and release them outside. "Reverence for life," the great missionary-doctor Albert Schweitzer called it.

For those of us who love the outdoors, perhaps Wilson summed up our feelings best: "Towns and farmland are the labyrinths that people have imposed between green wilderness sometime in the past, and we cherish the green enclaves accidentally left behind" (p. 6). Particularly in times of trouble, as I have lately discovered. Gazing out over a moonlit landscape in the wee hours of the night gives me a sense of peace and thanksgiving—a balm for my spirit. That is because, according to Wilson, "the natural world is the refuge of the spirit, remote, static, richer even than human imagination" (pp. 11–12). Furthermore, he believes that "humanity is exalted not because we are so far above other living creatures, but because knowing them well elevates the very concept of life" (p. 22).

If only our lumberman neighbor and all the other exploiters of nature's riches believed as Wilson does. A humble wonder, such as Wilson exhibits toward the natural world, must replace ruthless plunder before humanity's quality of life will improve. As it is now, we seem to be on an ever faster free-fall toward the destruction of life on earth as we know it. Like the seven does I found bedded down below our house early in the afternoon, seemingly unaware of hunting season, most people seem unaware of how dangerously close we are coming to irreparably damaging our life support system. The does are not connecting gunshots to their own possible demise; we are not connecting the earth's warning signals to our own possible extinction.

DECEMBER 17. We spent half of this lovely winter day walking over the lumberman's land with our retired forester friend. After looking carefully at the Soil Erosion Control Plan the lumberman had filed with the Soil Conservation office, he snorted in derision at the few "water bars" hastily constructed in steep sections of the skid roads. Running water had already broken through those inadequate barriers, and the roads were eroding fast. We also searched for the temporary culverts they had promised to put in at the three major stream crossings. There were none.

Then we asked him whether we could technically call the logging a clear-cut since a few scraggly trees had been left on the open knolls. Also, a small portion of the middle section of the property, primarily a thicket of grapevines and scrubby trees, had been ignored except for the removal of a few large trees near the top of the ridge. Our friend explained that a "clear-cut" is not necessarily defined as the total removal of every tree. Because nothing of value had been left in wide swathes on the mountainside, this *did* qualify as a clear-cut operation.

Carrying a video camera, he faithfully recorded the worst of the areas. And he agreed to testify on our behalf at the hearing. Our friend comes from the older generation of foresters who once cared about the land. He is distressed at the "new management" philosophy that has swept through the forest products industry—its almost total disregard for biodiversity and its overriding interest in profits first, for the CEO's and investors, but not for the workers and certainly not, on federal land, for the tax-payers who theoretically "own" the national forests. This seems to him to be a bastardizing of Gifford Pinchot's original "greatest good for the greatest amount of people" theory. "We used to care about the resource," he told us.

Despite his age—he retired a number of years ago—he is in remarkable condition and walked miles up and down the steep property to get the full picture. He also examined the slopes from our road and agreed on the dangers of sliding and erosion, especially given the disregard the loggers have already shown for environmentally sound "harvesting." Although he too noticed the reduction in wildlife—all we saw were American robins, a couple of ruffed grouse, and some does—he tried to comfort us with his deeply ingrained belief.

"This is a forgiving land," he said, "unlike the western United States where the soil is poorer and the climate drier. Give this several years, and many of the scars will be healed."

To some extent that is true, but unlike previous clear-cuts of the entire state, the forests now have to contend not only with continual soil loss and erosion, but with an artificially large number of deer that quickly consume new shoots, climate change due to global warming, as well as acid rain and other chemical pollutants in the air, water, and soil. According to the latest scientific estimates, if global warming is not curbed, what is left of natural Pennsylvania will be half grassland and half forests by 2050. Foresters who are looking ahead seem to be ignoring global warming and are confidently predicting that our forests over the next hundred years will be more diverse, with the *valuable* timber trees—primarily oaks—greatly reduced and replaced by a preponderance of red maples. They also predict a forest more like the one the original settlers discovered, excluding the American chestnut, of course, but otherwise having a greater number of hemlocks and white pines. "But," one forester confidently told me, "we'll just have to find new ways to use those trees."

In the meantime, as our forester friend said, "This is a great opportunity for you to observe the recovery processes of an eastern forest." He also advised me to monitor erosion by taking continual water samples and was pleased that I already had a baseline sampling from the last two years because of my participation in the Pennsylvania Alliance for Acid Rain monitoring. Every week I had collected water from our stream, first above the forks and then down at the big pulloff, and recorded both its acidity and its purity. Those figures might be useful if our stream degrades noticeably from the logging operation.

DECEMBER 18. The trees are dying in "Lucy's wood," the woods E. Lucy Braun named "mixed mesophytic" in 1916 when she was a young professor at the University of Cincinnati. As soon as I heard about it, I ran for the *Atlas of Pennsylvania*. How close was our woods to the mixed mesophytic? Not far, I quickly learned—only a county away. And many of the trees that grow in Lucy's woods also grow in ours: tulip, beech, basswood, sugar maple, hemlock, cucumber magnolia, and white, red, and black oak. But the mixed mesophytic is the oldest and most diverse deciduous forest region in North America, including southwestern Pennsylvania, southeastern Ohio, small portions of western Maryland and Virginia, most of West Virginia, eastern Kentucky, and a sliver through Tennessee and Alabama. Because it has never been glaciated or covered by the sea, and never formed part of the plains, it has been evolving for 60 million years. In addition, it has been blessed with abundant rain and warm weather.

But now, near Beckley, West Virginia, the trees are dropping over, their roots rotten, their bases swollen by extra cambium—the trees' "mortal attempt to make up for its rotted roots, which no longer function."[2] It began with the locust trees on dry ridge tops twenty years ago. Hickory trees were the next to succumb. Now, the red oaks are going fast.

The experts are puzzled. They don't know why the trees are dying in their prime. But there are theories—acid rain and excess ozone from high-compression engines and other sources are among the suspected causal agents. Researchers know that ozone is probably decreasing tree growth, but they did not expect major damage. At least one forest ecologist and acid-rain researcher, Orie L. Loucks, has been thinking deeply about the possible consequences to trees of excess ozone and nitrogen in the atmosphere. Put simply, such doses are too much for the trees to bear. They did not evolve in a highly industrial world and they cannot absorb the amount of stress our lifestyle is putting on them. So they are falling over, snapping off, curtailing their natural life cycle.[3] But still the experts and politicians argue. Dissenting foresters say that the mixed mesophytic forest is in excellent shape, more productive than ever.

Who do you believe in this day of experts challenging experts? Or, is it a case of the more they know, the less they understand? I can't help feeling that we have all become sorcerer's apprentices, in thrall to processes that we started with good intentions but are helpless to stop once they gain a momentum of their own.

DECEMBER 19. Nine degrees and crystal clear at dawn— a beautiful day to go to court at eight in the morning.

All of us were stunned at the proceedings. No testimony was allowed, so our forester and our geologist, the

2. Little, "Report from Lucy's Woods," p. 26.
3. Ibid., p. 68.

latter armed optimistically with charts and graphs to help make his points, could only listen as first our lawyer and then theirs presented their pleas.

Although he had the facts and figures and pressed the issues we were concerned about, our lawyer was meticulous with the truth. He emphasized our concern with the road's fragility and possible destruction because of the instability of the slopes, "their only access to their home." He also mentioned the compromise we thought we had reached to trade land nearly two years ago. But their forester had never carried through with the figures, he charged.

To my surprise, and contrary to what their lawyer had told our lawyer, the lumberman's former forester, a young graduate of the Penn State School of Forest Resources, was part of his support group. Months ago he had told us he no longer worked for the lumberman, so I had assumed that was why they were doing such a terrible job. Surely, no self-respecting forester would approve of such work. But there he sat, and we could see him protesting to their lawyer our lawyer's statement about the land swap. Was he or was he not working for the lumberman? Could what we were seeing actually be an example of a forester's counsel?

Because we had issued the first injunction and they had followed with their own injunction, demanding a key to our gate, our lawyer had to testify first. This gave our opponents an added advantage. Their lawyer could not only present his own testimony on their behalf but also "correct" statements our lawyer had made. And, of course, none of us could answer back. We had to sit there and listen as their lawyer, depending on a dramatic defense of his client's rights, proceeded to make statements that showed little or no understanding of what was involved.

Unlike our lawyer, who had taken the time to walk up our road and survey the situation, their lawyer had never seen the property, the road, or the slopes. Instead, he relied on what his client and his client's employees had told him. At least that was the only conclusion I could reach when time after time what he said did not accord with what had actually happened or the conditions of the property. But each time he covered himself by saying, "As I understand it," for instance, "As I understand it my client has not clear-cut the mountain," or, "As I understand it, the road is not a primitive cart road, but is capable of supporting oil delivery trucks." He also said that it was our fault the compromise had not gone through. Their forester had told us our proposed trade lands did not have enough lumber to compensate for not cutting the 200-foot area and that we would have to come up with more lumber, but we had never responded, he claimed. That was news to us. It also called into question the lumberman's denial on the phone to Bruce that the forester had ever marked the trees or met with Bruce.

The more their lawyer talked, the more the whole proceeding resembled Alice in Wonderland—totally unreal, mostly a confusion of events that bore little resemblance to what had actually happened over the years. Their lawyer neatly sidestepped the basic issue—the instability of the slope and our possible loss of access. Instead he went after us about not letting them have a key to the gate, conveniently neglecting to mention the many letters Bruce had written asking for help in maintaining the road. Certainly his use of metaphor was colorful although, as Bruce later pointed out, not entirely accurate.

"Mr. Bonta," he intoned in his best lawyerly voice, "has chosen to control the road." Recalling the old tale of the Three Billy Goats Gruff, he accused Bruce of being the "troll under the bridge, controlling the access."

He did make a few concessions, all of which we duly noted: "My client has an obligation to keep that road open. We don't want to use the road to timber. We have the same reasons to use the road as Mr. Bonta—with pickup trucks." But to our ears the best statement that he made was, "We don't own any land on the other side of the road and have no intention of cutting on that side." Then why, I asked silently, did your client have a surveyor prominently mark trees below the road with paint and slashes?

The crux of the whole business lay in his opening statement: "In Pennsylvania the law states that a man can do whatever he wants with his own land." And it was obvious that the judge agreed. He denied our injunction, saying that the issues were too complicated and he scheduled another hearing for February 26. And he granted their injunction—we were to give them a key to the gate. At first our friends and I thought that by setting another date, we had won. But Bruce and our lawyer informed us otherwise and our lawyer gave them a key. The lumberman, short, stocky, with a shock of white hair, stood grinning triumphantly like Alice's Cheshire cat. By the time the February 26 hearing took place, the hollow would be cleared.

Bitterly, I digested the lesson all of us had learned. Truth was not the issue in this court of law. Appearance was everything; substance counted for nothing. The fact that we lived on the mountain and they did not made no difference. Our safety, as we used the road during their timbering operation, was not important. But the convenience to their loggers of being able to use the road that we had been maintaining single-handedly for twenty-one years necessitated our giving them a key. Where was the justice in this?

No justice, I reminded myself. Not for us and certainly not for the land.

Unless the rights of private ownership are not only questioned but limited, there is no hope of saving the natural world and, in the end, ourselves. The majority of the earth's people, victims, rather than benefactors of exploitation, must finally say to the exploiters: "No. You are destroying everyone's inheritance, even on to the third and fourth generations. Your rights as landowners are not to exploit your land but to live in harmony with it. Otherwise, you forfeit your rights to ownership. You must be *responsible* stewards, not irresponsible pirates."

It was difficult to muster the energy to go outside later, despite the beautiful day. But such a day in the face of our defeat merely reinforced the neutrality of nature. Again I followed a trail of blood, this time along Laurel Ridge Trail. Some poor doe had met her end and was dragged for miles by a victorious hunter during the last hours of the last day of doe season.

The meek will not inherit the earth, as Jesus claimed. The greedy will, and the diversity of life forms will shrink more rapidly as the years pass. For a long time the land has been like God, who allows us to keep sinning against humanity and nature and yet keeps forgiving us. At some point, though, the land will wear out and God may grow tired of us.

DECEMBER 20. And yet! As autumn rolls inexorably toward winter, I find it difficult to believe that nature is less than invincible. I stood out on the veranda, clad in my bathrobe, listening to a screech owl trilling over and over from Sapsucker Ridge in the early morning light. Later I went outside to watch the sun rise over Sinking Valley. I welcomed the cold, clear air of winter and its infinite blue light slanting across the landscape.

Downy woodpeckers, white-breasted nuthatches, and black-capped chickadees, birds of winter, foraged across the Laurel Ridge Trail, and American crows cawed in the distance. Otherwise, the ridgetop was silent and no mammal moved. I liked to believe that they had consorted in the bright moonlight and were now resting in their burrows and shelters. The First Field thicket was filled with more winter birds—a flock of dark-eyed juncos and a pair of northern cardinals. Three American robins flew overhead calling.

Later, down in the hollow, a winter wren popped out at the forks. Below the big pulloff, a rustling noise on the bank alerted me to a foraging white-footed mouse poking its nose into exposed dried leaves, uncaring that I stood and watched as it scratched its long, white hind feet into crannies in search of seeds. Bright-eyed, with a long, slender tail, it had white underparts and feet and its round ears were pressed back against its head. Finally, it hustled up a tree trunk and out of sight.

Walking back up the road, I discovered a flock of golden-crowned kinglets along with brown creepers and tufted titmice. I sat and watched sixty pine siskins eating first the seeds of hemlock cones and then the seeds of black birch trees. The hollow road was sheltered and sunny; the stream water sparkled in the sunshine. It was still an exquisite place for beauty-loving humans and a bountiful place for hungry and thirsty wildlife.

DECEMBER 21. Thirty-two degrees at dawn with a new inch of heavy, frosting-on-the-cake snow coating every branch and twig—a wonderland snow that won't last long because of the wind, so I was out early to soak in the beauty. The valley below was still brown and drab-looking, clad in late autumn's colors. I heard no sound but the wind, which gradually lightened and brightened the sky, unveiling patches of blue between the scudding clouds. Fresh grouse, deer, and squirrel tracks crossed the trail at intervals. Two ruffed grouse exploded out from cover above the Far Field Road bank.

Near dusk I was drawn back down the hollow road for a final look before the loggers return. Below the big pull-off I noticed droppings on the road and looked up into a small hemlock tree growing out of the bank. There on a low branch sat a sleeping eastern screech owl. I spoke quietly to it, but still it slumbered. The light was dim and the owl too close for my binoculars. I moved off and sat against the bank watching. Still it was impossible to distinguish the owl's color. It remained motionless, eyes tightly shut, a dark silhouette in the branches.

After a while I tried clapping loudly and calling, but it continued to sleep. When at last I stood up and walked directly beneath the tree, the owl snapped awake and slowly swiveled its head around to watch me. I could see then that it was a red phase screech owl. To be regarded so closely by an owl, essence of all that is wild and beautiful, was an exhilarating conclusion to this bittersweet autumn.

Epilogue

My aspens dear, whose airy cages quelled
Quelled, or quenched in leaves the leaping sun,
All felled, felled, are all felled;
Of a fresh and following folded rank
Not spared, not one.

—Gerard Manley Hopkins, "Binsey Poplars"

Two days after Christmas, on a bleak, overcast day, the skidders and bulldozer returned, quickly reopening the Lower Road to the last hollow above the big pulloff. In the space of ten minutes, two huge trees were felled. I sat below, on our side of the road, blinking away tears as I watched them. What took nature centuries to create, men took only seconds to destroy.

As I continued watching, I tried to date the beginning of humanity's mastery of nature. Was it with the invention of the internal combustion engine or the development of the atomic bomb? When did technology overpower nature? Even through my binoculars, the yellow skidder looked as if it were driving itself, a faceless monster without a soul—a technological horror run amok. During their frenzied cutting that day, the logging crew dislodged an enormous stump end that tumbled down the slope and crashed into the third pulloff. Anyone standing below when it hurtled down the slope would have been killed.

It was then that we resolved to do the only thing we could—engage in peaceful monitoring. We would spend as much time as possible down in the hollow, armed only with a camera, a notebook, and pen. In reality, that meant I would be the major actor, a depressing and possibly dangerous job. Stubbornly I sat on our side of the road, ignoring the occasional harassing calls from the loggers. I also made certain they saw my camera as I clicked off photographs of their careless work.

First I photographed the stump. Then I photographed the slash remaining from several trees that had fallen across our road. With that ammunition Bruce wrote still another letter to the lumberman, warning of the "clear and present danger their work posed to us." He sent the letter certified mail so that the lumberman could not deny having ever received it. A couple of days later, the loggers were using cables and a winch to keep the trees from falling on the road. A minor, but satisfying victory.

Day after day the mayhem continued. The weather remained cooperative long after it should have. And I continued to be amazed at the efforts they were expending to cut, store, and haul out their booty. Often, the amount of gas, oil, and manpower they used to drag off a couple of large trees seemed counterproductive. For instance, one day two men with chain saws kept trying to cut enough of a fallen tree's branches so that its trunk could be released from the tangle of debris and dragged up the steep slope by the skidder. The engine continued rumbling away even after they successfully attached the log and all the men walked off for their hour lunch break. That tree was almost two miles away from the main yarding area near a paved road. Watching how much nonrenewable energy they used to make a few dollars was a lesson in how traditional economists still view our GNP, counting actual dollar profit without calculating the real cost in the permanent loss of resources and damage to the biosphere.

They worked on New Year's Day, continuing to cut all the usable trees along the side hollows, since most of those fell conveniently parallel to the road. And during one of our weekend inspections we found that many, but not all, of the big trees had been marked with blue paint, the first positive evidence we had that the forester might still be working for them. We also discovered a new, steep hauling road which had knee-deep, muddy ruts. Unaccountably, the weather continued not only mild but unseasonably warm, and the skidders turned the logging roads into a sucking quagmire.

Then, on January 8, I walked down the hollow road in early afternoon for my daily inspection. Three men were using the yellow skidder to try to haul logs up with cables, but they were having trouble getting the logs attached. At the second hollow above the big pulloff, I found a brown stream of water coming down out of their lumbering area and flowing into the main stream. As I looked down at the main stream, to the left it was brown, to the right above the muddy tributary, it was still its pristine self. The photographs I took then were dramatic, and I continued on down the road, snapping photograph after photograph of brown water down to the entrance of the hollow where the stream empties into the river.

Something snapped in me. I hurried home and called the Soil Conservation office. Trying to be as pleasant as I could, I asked politely if they ever reinspected an area for which they had already approved a Soil Erosion Control Plan. The lady told me that they rarely had enough staff to do so, but in the case of our neighbor's work they had planned to reinspect because of what Bruce had told them before the court hearing. We made an appointment for January 13.

The weather cooperated for once. It was nearly sixty degrees and clear, but the logging roads were so mired in mud that the loggers could not work. That enabled me to take the Soil Conservation inspector all over their land, pointing out their violations—no visible culverts at stream crossings, evidence of skidders running directly up a streambed, the knee-deep ruts, and the steep new roads running with muddy water. It didn't take her long to agree with me that their Soil Erosion Control Plan was totally worthless and that they would have to revise it. Still, she said, there was little that they could legally do to force the loggers to comply. Unlike coal mining, which is strictly regulated, logging is almost totally unregulated.

"Funny thing," she added. "The people in logging are the ones who set up minimal standards—design the Soil Erosion Control Plans and sit on the county conservation boards that oversee logging operations. It's like the fox guarding the henhouse." Such practices are becoming more, not less, common, she added. So even if she sent her recommendations to the lumberman, he didn't have to comply. But she promised to do her best.

And she did. She fired off a letter immediately which said, in effect, that he was violating the law by "polluting the waters of the Commonwealth." She also asked for an update on his Soil Erosion Control Plan, telling him she had recently reinspected the property and found more roads and more logging than his plan had called for. It was a fierce letter and proved to be the turning point in the whole depressing affair. No more trees were cut, not even those with blue spots. In two days all the previously cut trees were hauled off, and a week later, on a bitterly cold Sunday, I encountered potential purchasers of our neighbor's property walking up the road to inspect it.

Over the next four months, a friend who had agreed to act on our behalf outbid all the other buyers and the land was ours. Although Bruce had offered to pay more than any other bidder, the lumberman, as Bruce has suspected, refused to sell to us. But how he liked our friend!

After he considered his bids and told our friend his was the highest, the lumberman then raised the price $5,000 more. Our friend remained firm, and a few months later the lumberman called to say the deed was ready.

So now we own it all. Sixty percent of the hollow remains untouched, and no more skidders or chain saws will invade it during our lifetimes. By using the few meager weapons we could muster, we saved the road bank garlanded in ephemeral wildflowers as well as the large trees below the road. If we avert our eyes, we can still imagine the hollow as it once was and celebrate the leftovers now that the feasting has ended. Like environmentalists everywhere, we were forced to conclude that a small portion of a loaf was better than none.

Given a little luck, the mountainside will not slide down on our road, and green shoots will reclaim the degraded slopes. Not without our help however. During the weeks after we finally got the deed in July, Bruce explored the devastated areas and discovered that there was no grass growing on the main haul road up Sapsucker Ridge to control erosion, despite the commitment in the lumberman's Soil Erosion Control Plan that grass seed would be planted. Although Pennsylvania smartweed had quickly grown up along many of the skid trails, the steep haul road was still bare of vegetation in August and eroding badly. The water bars they had put in had already been breached, and it was obvious that soil erosion was continuing at a rapid rate. Bruce quickly bought the seed mixture specified in their plan, planted the haul road, and re-dug the water bars by hand. We will continue to do what we can to help the land heal over into some semblance of its former self, and even though, in our lifetimes, the hollow will not regain its former splendor, we hope to preserve it for future generations.

In the spring, after the prolonged season of rapine and pillage, the uncut portion of the hollow bloomed again. Louisiana waterthrushes sang up and down the stream. Purple trillium crowded the stream bank. Rue anemone, hepatica, and woodland violets carpeted the roadside. The neotropical migrants returned in force: wood thrushes, worm-eating warblers, ovenbirds, scarlet tanagers, black-throated green warblers, rose-breasted grosbeaks, and eastern wood pewees. But we wondered how successful their nesting was since the clear-cut above has opened up the once unbroken forest, creating a habitat known to be deleterious to deep woods' nesters, but attractive to a wide variety of nest predators—common grackles, blue jays, raccoons, skunks—and to the infamous brown-headed cowbird which lays its eggs in the nests of neotropical migrants to the detriment of their own nestlings. Will we continue to see those increasingly rare songbirds in the years to come? And how will the clearing influence the lives of the deep hollow trees still standing? Open now to the harsh winds, will they continue to topple and further degrade the hollow?

But there is no doubt about the effects in the clear-cut area. In the piles of slash above and out on the open knolls, no birds sang. It is a wasteland, its bones picked clean by vultures, its once sparkling streamlets choked with debris—a paradigm for what the entire earth will become if we do not change our ways.

I wept for what had been and what will never be again.

Selected Bibliography
Index

Selected Bibliography

General

Armstrong, Edward A. *St. Francis: Nature Mystic*. Berkeley and Los Angeles: University of California Press, 1973.

Barron, George. "Jekyll-Hyde Mushrooms." *Natural History* 101 (March 1992): 46–53.

Bonta, Mark. *Bioplum: A Biological Inventory of the Bonta Property and Adjacent Parcels Northern Brush Mountain, Blair County, Pennsylvania*. Plummer's Hollow, Pa.: 1991.

Borland, Hal. *Hill Country Harvest*. Philadelphia: J. P. Lippincott & Sons, 1967.

Bowden, Charles. *Frog Mountain Blues*. Tucson: University of Arizona Press, 1987.

Brooks, Maurice. *The Appalachians*. Boston: Houghton Mifflin, 1965.

Burroughs, John. *Signs and Seasons*. Boston: Houghton Mifflin, 1886.

Cuff, David J., Edward K. Muller, William J. Young, Wilbur Zelinsky, and Ronald F. Abler. *The Atlas of Pennsylvania*. Philadelphia: Temple University Press, 1989.

Diamond, Jared. *The Third Chimpanzee: The Evolution and Future of the Human Animal*. New York: Harper Collins, 1992.

Jerome, John. *Stone Work: Reflections on Serious Play and Other Aspects of Country Life*. New York: Viking Press, 1989.

Kalm, Peter. *Travels in North America*. New York: Dover Publications, 1987.

Krieger, Louis C. C. *The Mushroom Handbook*. New York: Dover Publications, 1967.

Leopold, Aldo. *A Sand County Almanac*. New York: Oxford University Press, 1966.

Lopez, Barry. *The Rediscovery of North America*. Lexington: University Press of Kentucky, 1990.

Martin, Calvin Luther. *In the Spirit of the Earth: Rethinking History and Time*. Baltimore: Johns Hopkins University Press, 1992.

Matthews, Albert. "The Term Indian Summer." *Monthly Weather Review* 30 (1902): 19–28.

Miller, Jr., Orson K. *Mushrooms of North America*. New York: Dutton, 1979.

Nash, James A. *Loving Nature: Ecological Integrity and Christian Responsibility.* Nashville: Abingdon Press, 1991.

Nelson, Richard K. *The Island Within.* San Francisco: North Point Press, 1989.

Peattie, Donald Culross. *An Almanac for Moderns.* Boston: David R. Godine, 1980.

Phillips, Catherine, ed. *Gerard Manley Hopkins.* Oxford: Oxford University Press, 1986.

Snyder, Gary. *Riprap; and, Cold Mountain poems.* San Francisco: North Point Press, 1990.

Thoreau, Henry David. *Walden.* New York: Bramhall House, 1951.

White, Jr., Lynn. "The Historical Roots of Our Ecologic Crisis." *Science* 155 (March 10, 1967): 1203–07.

Wilson, Edward O. *Biophilia: The Human Bond with Other Species.* Cambridge, Mass.: Harvard University Press, 1984.

Birds

Baker, Robin. *The Mystery of Migration.* New York: Viking Press, 1981.

Bent, Arthur Cleveland. *Life Histories of North American Birds of Prey.* 2 vols. New York: Dover Publications, 1961.

———. *Life Histories of North American Cardinals, Grosbeaks, Buntings, Towhees, Finches, Sparrows and Their Allies.* 3 vols. New York: Dover Publications, 1968.

———. *Life Histories of North American Nuthatches, Wrens, Thrashers, and Their Allies.* New York: Dover Publications, 1964.

Bonta, Marcia. "Project FeederWatch." *Birder's World* 4 (Oct. 1990): 19.

Fisher, James, and Roger Tory Peterson. *The World of Birds.* Garden City, N.Y.: Doubleday, 1964.

Fitzpatrick, John W. "Northern Birds at Home in the Tropics." *Natural History* 91 (Sept. 1982): 40–47.

Forbush, E. H., and John Richard May. *Natural History of the Birds of Eastern and Central North America.* Boston: Houghton Mifflin, 1939.

Gullion, Gordon. *The Ruffed Grouse.* Minocqua, Wis.: North Wood Press, 1989.

Holroyd, Geoffrey L., and John G. Woods. "Migration of the Saw-Whet Owl in Eastern North America." *Birdbanding* 46 (Spring 1975): 101–05.

Kilham, Lawrence. *The American Crow and the Common Raven.* College Station: Texas A & M University Press, 1989.

Middleton, Alex L. "Seasonal Changes in Plumage Structure and Body Composition of American Goldfinch." *Canadian Field-Naturalist* 100 (Oct.–Dec. 1986): 545–49.

Munn, Charles A. "Birds of Different Feather Also Flock Together." *Natural History* 93 (Nov. 1984): 34–42.

Murphy, Pat. "Quick Takes." *Bird Watcher's Digest* 8 (Sept.–Oct. 1985): 6.

Nickell, Walter P. "Studies of Habitats, Territory, and Nests of the Eastern Goldfinch." *The Auk* 68 (1951): 447–70.

Parkes, Kenneth C. "Family Tree." *Birder's World* 5 (August 1991): 34–37.

Peterson, Roger Tory. *A Field Guide to the Birds of Eastern and Central North American*. Boston: Houghton Mifflin, 1980.

Sabine, Winifred S. "Flight Behavior of a Flock of Slate-Colored Juncos in the Late Afternoon." *The Auk* 74 (1957): 391.

Stanwood, Cordelia. Papers. Stanwood Wildlife Sanctuary. Ellsworth, Maine.

Stokes, Donald W. *A Guide to Bird Behavior: Volume I*. Boston: Little, Brown, 1979.

Stokes, Donald W., and Lillian Q. Stokes. *A Guide to Bird Behavior: Volume II*. Boston: Little, Brown, 1983.

———. *A Guide to Bird Behavior: Volume III*. Boston: Little, Brown, 1989.

Terborgh, John. *Where Have All the Birds Gone?* Princeton: Princeton University Press, 1989.

Terres, John K. *The Audubon Society Encyclopedia of North American Birds*. New York: Alfred A. Knopf, 1982.

Williams, Janet M. "That Divine Impulse." *The Living Bird Quarterly* 3 (Autumn 1984): 8–12.

Wood, Merrill. *Birds of Central Pennsylvania: The State College Region*. State College, Pa.: State College Bird Club, 1983.

Forests and Forestry

Baker, F. S. *Principles of Silviculture*. New York: McGraw-Hill, 1950.

Blymer, M. J., and B. S. McGinnes. "Observations of Possible Detrimental Effects of Clearcutting on Terrestrial Amphibians." *Bulletin of the Maryland Herpetological Society* 13 (1977): 79–83.

Bolgiano, Chris. "A Case for Eastern Old-Growth." *American Forests* 95 (May–June 1989): 26–31, 48.

Duffy, David Cameron, and Albert J. Meier. "Do Appalachian Herbaceous Understories Ever Recover from Clearcutting?" *Conservation Biology* 6 (June 1992): 196–201.

Laycock, George. "Old-Time Logging Makes a Comeback." *Audubon* 93 (Sept.–Oct. 1991): 110–15.

Little, Charles E. "Report from Lucy's Woods." *American Forests* 98 (March–April 1992): 25–27, 68–69.

Manes, Christopher. "In Praise of Yew." *Orion* 11 (Winter 1992): 30–39.

Manning, Richard. *Last Stand Logging, Journalism and the Case for Humility.* Salt Lake City: Gibbs-Smith, 1991.

Minckler, Leon S. "Group Selection Beats Clearcutting in the Eastern Hardwoods." *Forest Watch* 12 (Oct. 1991): 21–31.

O'Donnell, Ellen. *Forest Stewardship—Our Link to the Past—Our Legacy for the Future.* State College: College of Agricultural Sciences, School of Forest Resources, Pennsylvania State University, 1992.

Pough, F. Harvey, Ellen M. Smith, Donald H. Rhodes, and Andres Collazo. "The Abundance of Salamanders in Forest Stands with Different Histories of Disturbance." *Forest Ecology and Management* 20 (1987): 1–9.

Robinson, Gordon. *The Forest and the Trees: A Guide to Excellent Forestry.* Washington, D.C.: Island Press, 1988.

———. "The Sierra Club Position on Clear-Cutting and Forest Management." *Sierra Club Bulletin* 56 (Feb. 1971): 14–17.

Stone, Christopher D. *Should Trees Have Standing? Toward Legal Rights for Natural Objects.* Palo Alto, Calif.: Tioga Press, 1988.

Zuckerman, Seth. "Old Forestry: A Visit to California's Collins Almanor Forest, a Logging Operation with a Future." *Sierra* 77 (March–April 1992): 44.

———. *Saving Our Ancient Forests.* Venice, California: Living Planet Press, 1991.

Insects

Borror, Donald J., and Richard E. White. *A Field Guide to the Insects of America North of Mexico.* Boston: Houghton Mifflin, 1970.

Brower, Lincoln P. "A Royal Voyage to an Enchanted Forest." *Orion* 6 (Summer 1987): 26–35.

Comstock, John Henry, and Anna Botsford Comstock. *A Manual for the Study of Insects.* Ithaca, N.Y.: Comstock Publishing Co., 1904.

Emerton, James H. *The Common Spiders of the United States.* New York: Dover Publications, 1961.

Evans, Howard Ensign. *Wasp Farm.* New York: Anchor Press, 1973.

George, Jean Craighead. "My Search for Secret Agent #25238." *National Wildlife* 16 (April–May 1978): 16–19.

Hutchins, Ross E. *Insects.* Englewood Cliffs, N.J.: Prentice-Hall, 1966.

Opler, Paul A., and Vichai Malikul. *Eastern Butterflies*. Boston: Houghton Mifflin, 1992.

Stokes, Donald W. *A Guide to Observing Insect Lives*. Boston: Little, Brown, 1983.

Teale, Edwin Way. *Grassroot Jungles*. New York: Dodd, Mead, 1937.

———. *Near Horizons*. New York: Dodd, Mead, 1942.

Wheeler, A. G., Jr. "Locust Leafminer, *Odontata dorsalis* (Thunberg)." *Regulatory Horticulture*. Entomology Circular No. 115, Pennsylvania Department of Agriculture, Bureau of Plant Industry, Fall 1987.

Mammals

Jacobs, Lucia. "Cache Economy of the Gray Squirrel." *Natural History* 98 (Oct. 1989): 40–45.

Merritt, Joseph F. *Guide to the Mammals of Pennsylvania*. Pittsburgh: University of Pittsburgh Press, 1987.

Rue, Leonard Lee, III. *The Deer of North America*. Danbury, Conn.: Grolier Book Clubs, 1989.

Wishner, Lawrence. *Eastern Chipmunks: Secrets of Their Solitary Lives*. Washington, D.C.: Smithsonian Institution Press, 1982.

Plants

Björkman, Erik. "Monotropa Hypopitys L.—An Epiparasite on Tree Roots." *Physiologia Plantarum* 13 (1960): 308–27.

Blanchan, Neltje. *Wild Flowers: An Aid to Knowledge of Our Wild Flowers and Their Insect Visitors*. New York: Doubleday, Page, 1916.

Cobb, Boughton. *A Field Guide to the Ferns*. Boston: Houghton Mifflin, 1956.

Comstock, Anna B. *Trees at Leisure*. Ithaca, N.Y.: Comstock Publishing Company, 1916.

Durant, Mary. *Who Named the Daisy? Who Named the Rose? A Roving Dictionary of North American Wildflowers*. New York: Congdon & Weed, 1976.

Grimm, William Carey. *The Shrubs of Pennsylvania*. Harrisburg: Stackpole and Heck, 1952.

———. *The Trees of Pennsylvania*. Harrisburg: Stackpole and Heck, 1950.

Kuijt, Job. *The Biology of Parasitic Flowering Plants*. Berkeley and Los Angeles: University of California Press, 1969.

Peattie, Donald Culross. *A Natural History of Trees of Eastern and Central North America*. 2d edition. New York: Bonanza Books, 1966.

Peterson, Roger Tory, and Margaret McKenny. *A Field Guide to Wild-flowers of Northeastern and Northcentral North America.* Boston: Houghton Mifflin, 1968.

Rickett, Harold William. *Wildflowers of the Northeastern States.* 2 vols. New York: McGraw Hill, 1966.

Scott, Jane. *Botany in the Field: An Introduction to Plant Communities for the Amateur Naturalist.* Englewood Cliffs, N.J.: Prentice-Hall, 1984.

Stiles, Edmund W. "Fruit for All Seasons." *Natural History* 93 (August 1984): 42–53.

Swain, Roger. "The Fungus Connection." *Horticulture* 57 (August 1979): 16–17.

Reptiles and Amphibians

Babcock, Harold L. *Turtles of the Northeastern United States.* New York: Dover Publications, 1971.

Conant, Roger, and Joseph T. Collins. *Reptiles and Amphibians Eastern/Central North America.* Boston: Houghton Mifflin, 1991.

Shaffer, Larry L. *Pennsylvania Amphibians and Reptiles.* Harrisburg: Pennsylvania Fish Commission, 1991.

Index

PITT SERIES IN NATURE AND NATURAL HISTORY
Marcia Bonta, Editor

Amphibians and Reptiles in West Virginia
Bayard N. Green and Thomas K. Pauley

Appalachian Autumn
Marcia Bonta

Appalachian Spring
Marcia Bonta

Atlas of Breeding Birds in Pennsylvania
Daniel W. Brauning, Editor

Buck Fever: The Deer Hunting Tradition in Pennsylvania
Mike Sajna

Guide to the Mammals of Pennsylvania
Joseph F. Merritt

Rattler Tales from Northcentral Pennsylvania
C. E. Brennan

Soldiers Delight Journal: Exploring a Globally Rare Ecosystem
Jack Wennerstrom

The West Virginia Breeding Bird Atlas
Albert R. Buckelew, Jr., and George A. Hall

Youghiogheny: Appalachian River
Tim Palmer